Jews and Christians; becoming friends

Gervase Vernon

DEDICATION

For the Jews of Bobowa murdered by the Nazis
in Garbacz forest on August 14, 1942

f

CONTENTS

ACKNOWLEDGMENTS

Many thanks to Stan Keller, the chairman of the Chelmsford Jewish community, who spoke on the course about the Holocaust. Thanks also to the Anglican Diocese of Chelmsford, who ran the course during Lent 2023 and, in particular to Diane Hardy who organised it and Hazel Kempton who dealt with the video-conferencing technology. Thanks to the the course participants, some of whose suggestions have been incorporated into this written version. Finally, I am grateful to Claire Malone-Lee, a friend and a scholar of Christian-Jewish relations, for her illuminating comments

FRONT COVER

The front cover shows the miniature entitled 'The Jewish notables before King Casimir the Great' from Arthur Szyk's 1927 book of miniatures, 'The Statute of Kalisz'. In 1264 the statute of Kalisz placed the relations between Jews and gentiles in Poland on a legal basis for the first time. Arthur Szyk, a Polish Jewish artist, had been commissioned by the Second Polish Republic to produce a set of miniatures celebrating this statute. The miniatures were exhibited throughout Poland in an attempt to improve relations between Jewish and gentile Poles. This particular sheet is a first impression dedicated to Szyk's friend, my grandfather General Bolesław Wieniawa Długoszowski. The reason for using this miniature as a cover is to demonstrate the long history of efforts to place relations between Jews and gentiles in Poland on a legal and equitable basis. More about the details of the illustration can be found in my book '*Belonging and Betrayal*'.

1 INTRODUCTION

This booklet is based on a five-week course on Christianity and Judaism given alongside Stan Keller, the chairman of the Chelmsford Jewish community, under the auspices of the Anglican Diocese of Chelmsford, during Lent 2023. Some suggestions from the course participants have been incorporated into this written version. I am also grateful to Claire Malone-Lee, a friend and a scholar of Christian-Jewish relations, for her many illuminating comments. It is offered to other Christian churches and local Jewish communities who wish to undergo a similar journey.

It is easy to say what this course is not. It is not a scholarly work. It is obviously not a comprehensive study of the relationship between Christianity and Judaism. A brief bibliography suggesting further reading can be found at the end. It is not 'scriptural reasoning' as pioneered by David F Ford and others because, sadly, all the participants, with the exception of Stan Keller, were Christians.[1] It is, on the other hand, an example of receptive ecumenism. The emphasis, in other words, is on understanding the other, Judaism in this case, in order to appreciate it better. Knowing the faith of Jews better, to paraphrase Richard of Chichester's famous prayer,[2] we can know them better and love them better. The emphasis is not on using Jewish sources to understand Christianity better.

I myself am a Christian and a member of the Roman Catholic church. However, my mother, herself half-Jewish, came from a village in Poland, Bobowa (Bobov in Yiddish) where almost all the Jews were killed during the second world war. A study of Christianity and Judaism is not, then, for me purely an intellectual pursuit, but an attempt to address wounds deep within myself and within European society.

---

[1] David F. Ford, Regius Professor of Divinity at Cambridge. The Promise of Scriptural Reasoning. Ed. with C. C. Pecknold. With chapter 'An Inter-Faith Wisdom: Scriptural Reasoning between Jews, Christians and Muslims' at pp. 1–22 (Blackwell, Oxford, 2006)
See also; Jews, Christians and Muslims Meet around their Scriptures: An Inter-faith Practice for the 21st Century. Professor David F. Ford. The Fourth Pope John Paul II Annual Lecture on Interreligious Understanding. The Pontifical University of St Thomas Aquinas 'Angelicum' with The Russell Berrie Foundation. Rome, April 5th 2011
https://www.interfaith.cam.ac.uk/resources/lecturespapersandspeeches/jewschristiansandmuslimsmeetaroundtheirscriptures

[2] [Jesus] 'O most merciful redeemer, friend and brother,
may I know thee more clearly,
love thee more dearly,
and follow thee more nearly, day by day.'

How this booklet works

The course is divided into five sections designed to be worked through a week apart by a group meeting together in person or by video conference. The first week looks at Jonathan Sack's commentary on Genesis and the second at his commentary on Exodus. **(PowerPoint presentations on which chapters 1 and 2 are based and which can be used by study groups, are to be found on Dropbox.)**[3]

In the third week Stan Keller (chairman of the Chelmsford Jewish community) talked about the Holocaust. The fourth week looks at how Christian anti-Judaism contributed to the Holocaust. Finally, the fifth week is a Bible study on Romans 9-11, the chapters where Paul most comprehensively deals with the relations between Christians and Jews, relations which caused him great agony of soul.[4]

Purpose of the booklet

The primary purpose of this course is to know God better and to love him better, through contemporary Jewish interpretations of the

---

[3] Exodus:
https://www.dropbox.com/s/qyxvurlvedus4cy/Exodus%20for%20Lent%20course.pptx?dl=0
Genesis:
https://www.dropbox.com/s/h3t1bps3pv6z9tz/Genesis%20for%20Lent%20course.pptx?dl=0
[4] An earlier version of week 5 was given as a talk at 'Breakfast with the Bible' in Chelmsford Anglican cathedral.

Hebrew Bible, and through re-interpretations of the New Testament inspired by these Jewish interpretations.

The secondary purpose of the booklet is to know and love better our 'elder brother' the community of Jews and those who belong to it.

Postscript

At the end of this booklet, for those who are interested, I have added a very short essay on the history of rabbinical Judaism, and on the interaction of Christianity, Judaism and secular philosophy over the ages. Finally I have added a short hand-out by Eva Mroczek, a scholar of ancient Judaism, which eloquently puts to bed the old view that one can contrast a 'Mean, Angry Old Testament God with a Nice, Loving New Testament God.'

2. WEEK 1, THE BOOK OF GENESIS

(The material about the purpose of the course, delivered in the first week, repeats much that is in the introduction.)

A The Purpose of this course

1)   The primary purpose of this course is to know God better and to love him better, through contemporary Jewish interpretations of the Hebrew Bible, and through re-interpretations of the New Testament inspired by these Jewish interpretations .

We will look at Jonathan Sack's commentary on Genesis in week 1 and on Exodus in week 2.

2)   The secondary purpose of this course is to know and love better our 'elder brother' the community of Jews and those who belong to it. The technical term for this approach, which has been used in ecumenical dialogue between Christian denominations, is receptive ecumenism. However, here we will attempt to use receptive ecumenism in the dialogue between Christianity and

Judaism. Receptive ecumenism simply means getting to know the other better in order to understand them better and love them better. It is to be contrasted with an ecumenism that looks for points of similarity in order to bring people together, or looks to learn from the experience of another group in order to enhance our understanding of our own faith. These are other approaches that can also be valuable and will be used on occasion in this booklet.

Week 3 is to be used to give the local Jewish community an opportunity to talk about the Holocaust to the participants. If this is truly not possible I have supplied an essay based on the experience of the holocaust in the village of Bobowa, Poland, from which my mother came. Week 4 is about how Christian anti-Judaism contributed to the Holocaust. The course finishes in week 5 with a Bible study on Romans 9-11.

B The structure of the course

1. Anything said in these sessions is confidential.
2. Each session is one hour, with about 20 minutes of prepared material and 40 minutes for interaction, so that the topics can be explored together.
3. The material can be sent to course participants before each weekly session, but without the expectation that it will be read by all participants. Nor will there be any expectation that the leader will reach the end of the prepared material each session.

4. This is emphatically not an exhaustive or scholarly study of this immense topic. Some background material, which will interest those who wish to take things further, can be found in the brief bibliography at the end.

C Prayer Before starting each weekly session

1. 'In Judaism, Faith is a form of listening – to the song creation sings to its creator, and to the message history delivers to those who strive to understand it. That is what Moses says time and again in Deuteronomy: Stop looking; listen. Stop speaking; listen. Create a silence in the soul. Still the clamour of instinct, desire, fear, anger. Strive to listen to the still, small voice beneath the noise. Then you will know that the universe is the work of One beyond the furthest star yet closer to you than you are to yourself – and then you will love the Lord.'[5]

2. May both Christians and Jews turn to you, God, whose gentleness and mercy is proclaimed throughout the Hebrew scriptures (the OT) and the New Testament.

Session 1

Introduction, structure and prayer, as above, then:

Exercise 1

Share something about yourself and your interest in this course. Some participants in the course may be interested because of

---

[5] From Jonathan Sacks, 'Covenant and conversation, Deuteronomy' Chapter 3, Va'ethanan, 'The meanings of Shema', p.60

Jewish roots or friends, some for other reasons. Only share with the group what you are happy to share. At least 20 minutes should be allowed for this exercise.

A summary of Genesis according to Jonathan Sacks[6]

1) The problem that has pre-occupied the Torah since the beginning is, 'how to achieve, in human affairs, a combination of freedom and order.'

2) In the beginning, God created order. Then he created humanity, endowing it with his greatest gift: freedom. But humans used freedom to damage, even destroy, the order God had created in the world. First, Adam and Eve eat the forbidden fruit. Then Cain, the first human child, commits the first murder. With breathtaking speed, humanity, by the eve of the flood, had turned the world into a place full of violence. For a moment, God 'regretted that he had made man on earth'. (Gen. 6:6). Human beings had reduced the world to freedom without order – in a word, chaos.

3) God commands Abraham to leave Mesopotamia and live a different kind of life in a different kind of land. Yet throughout Genesis, Abraham's descendants are only an extended family, not yet a nation capable of building a society. And, as Genesis makes clear, even the most

---

[6] Jonathan Sacks. *Genesis, the Book of Beginnings (v. 1) (Covenant and Conversation)*. Toby Press Ltd, 2010.

faithful family cannot avoid the impact of violence and chaos. Lot discovers this in Sodom. Abraham and Isaac encounter societies in which they fear for their lives because of the attractiveness of their wives. An example of this is when Jacob's daughter Diana is raped and abducted. By the end of Genesis, we understand why God has promised the patriarchs a land and so many descendants that they can form a nation. Only in a just society (a nation, not a family) can justice flourish. Only in a free society can individual liberty be sustained. That is why the Torah is a formula for the construction of a just society, not (primarily) a roadmap for the salvation of the soul.'[7]

Four topics from Genesis for discussion

Below are just brief notes to start the discussion.

1. The theme of the two sons in Genesis

Genesis kicks off with Adam who has two sons: Cain kills Abel.

Abraham has two sons, Isaac banishes Ismael, though they both appear at Abraham's funeral.

Isaac has two sons: Jacob and Esau. Jacob tricks Esau out of his inheritance, though again there is some reconciliation when Jacob returns to meet Esau.

---

[7] This summary of the book of Genesis is from Sacks, Deuteronomy, Shofetim, the three crowns p.127.

Jacob has twelve sons, but they sell Joseph into slavery in Egypt. Here, for the first time, there is full forgiveness when Joseph, now a governor in Egypt, forgives his brothers saying, 'you meant this for evil, but God meant it for good' (Genesis 50:20).

Genesis is the story of two sons – on each occasion God favours the younger son. On each successive occasion, the quality of reconciliation improves.

2. Psalm 133

Verse 1. 'Behold, how good and pleasant it is when brothers live together in harmony!

Verse 2. It is like fine oil on the head, running down on the beard, running down Aaron's beard over the collar of his robes.'

But who is Aaron's brother? It is, of course, Moses.

This psalm, then, is about the perfect unity between Moses and Aaron. This perfect unity between two brothers does not occur until the book of Exodus, but this is the destination towards which the gradually improving stories of the two brothers in Genesis are moving. For Sacks, this is also about the relationship between priest and prophet in Israel. Aaron was the priest, his brother Moses, the prophet. For Sacks, that relationship was key to the thriving of Israel. The priest is chosen by society and maintains society's ritual order. The prophet is appointed by God alone and calls people and priests back to God's commandments when they have strayed. The ideal harmony of priest and prophet is described and celebrated in Psalm 133.

New Testament
Exercise two

Identify the theme of the two brothers in the NT.

The prodigal son

The parable starts, 'there was a man who had two sons' (Luke 15:11). It should probably be called 'the parable of the two sons', not 'the prodigal son'.

Luke provides his interpretation of this parable. The passage begins, 'The Pharisees and scribes complained saying, "This man [Jesus] welcomes sinners and eats with them"' (Luke 15:3). This parable is Jesus's answer to their unspoken question, 'Why do you eat with sinners?' Note that in the story, the father, often taken to be standing for God, first welcomes the sinful prodigal son, then eats with him just as the Pharisees complain that Jesus welcomes sinners and eats with them.

But then, in this story, the father turns to the elder son and pleads with him too. The story is left open-ended because Jesus is pleading with the scribes and Pharisees. It is their response, it is our response, which will provide the ending.

Exercise three.

Share your interpretations of the prodigal son.

D The Noahide covenant and the council of Jerusalem

In Acts 15:19-21 there is a dispute between those who wanted gentile converts to Christianity to follow the whole Mosaic Law, including circumcision, and those, like Paul, who did not. James, the brother of Jesus and the leader of the Jerusalem community, makes these concluding remarks;

"It is my judgment, therefore, that we should not make it difficult for the Gentiles who are turning to God.

Instead, we should write to them, telling them to abstain from food polluted by idols, from sexual immorality, from the meat of strangled animals and from blood.

For the law of Moses has been preached in every city from the earliest times and is read in the synagogues on every Sabbath."

While the Noahide covenant (Genesis 9:4-6) is rarely mentioned in Christian theology, it has a considerable place in Rabbinic Judaism. In Rabbinic Judaism, the Noahide covenant, a covenant between God and all of humanity, given to Noah after the flood, and much elaborated in the Talmud,[8] is said to contain all the moral laws that non-Jews should follow. Non-Jews are not obligated to follow the Torah or convert to Judaism. The Torah is given to the Jews alone.

---

[8] Babylonian Talmud Sanhedrin 56a-b

James, in the passage above, appears to be taking a very similar position. The Gentiles, as non-Jews, do not have to follow the whole Mosaic Law, but only something very like the Noahide covenant.

3. WEEK 2. A JEWISH PERSPECTIVE ON THE BOOK OF EXODUS

God as both liberator and educator in Rabbi Jonathan Sacks's commentary on Exodus

Prayer (as week 1)

'In Judaism Faith is a form of listening – to the song creation sings to its creator, and to the message history delivers to those who strive to understand it. That is what Moses says time and again in Deuteronomy: Stop looking; listen. Stop speaking; listen. Create a silence in the soul. Still the clamour of instinct, desire, fear, anger. Strive to listen to the still, small voice beneath the noise. Then you will know that the universe is the work of One beyond the furthest star yet closer to you than you are to yourself – and then you will love the Lord.'[9]

---

[9] From Jonathan Sacks, 'Covenant and conversation, Deuteronomy' Chapter 3, Va'ethanan, 'The meanings of Shema', p.60

May both Christians and Jews turn to you, God, whose gentleness and mercy are proclaimed throughout the Hebrew scriptures (the OT) and the New Testament.

List of topics in this chapter about the book of Exodus

1) The structure of the book
2) The text, God (and Moses) as liberator
3) The subtext; God (and Moses) as educator
4) Israel as a signal of transcendence
5) Six compassionate women in Exodus
6) How does the book of Exodus help us understand the NT? (Structures and themes)
7) The sanctuary as the type of Christ

1) The structure of the book of Exodus, according to Rabbi Sacks

Exodus, as many OT works, has a chiastic structure. The theme of the first section is repeated in the last section, the theme of the second section is repeated in the penultimate section and so on. The themes run: ABCBA.

There are two arcs, the first arc is political.

	Topic	Chapter
A	Unjust society	1–6

B	Liberation: ten plagues	7–13
C	Division of the Red sea	14–18
B	Liberty: ten commandments	19–20
A	Just society	21–24

and it is followed by the second arc which is spiritual.

	Topic	Chapter
A	Tabernacle instruction	25–31:11
B	Sabbath	31:12-18
C	Golden calf	32–34
B	Sabbath	35:1-3
A	Tabernacle construction	35:4-40

Chiastic structures are omnipresent in the Pentateuch (first five books of the OT, called by Jews the Torah), not just in whole books, but in individual speeches.[10] The modern reader searches

---

[10] A website that lists and explains chiastic structures in the scriptures. This website focuses on the NT but contains some OT examples. https://www.chiasmusxchange.com/explanatory-notes/#:~:text=Chiasmus%20refers%20to%20a%20sequence,not%20man%20of

for a punchline at the end of a passage. Such punchlines can be found in the parables of Jesus who, in this respect stands as a modern man. But in a book or story with a chiastic structure, the 'punchline', or moment of high drama, is in the middle. In the first chiastic arc of Exodus, this moment of high drama is the division of the Red Sea. In the second arc, the moment of high drama is the episode of the Golden Calf.

2) The Text: God (and Moses) as liberator

The book of Exodus is a tale of God forming a nation, as promised to Abraham 400 years earlier, by taking a group of slaves out of Egypt. It is a tale of liberation from oppression. But it is also a description of the setting up of a new covenantal society. A covenantal society is a society where all people agree voluntarily to enter and, having entered the society, to follow its God-based rules. In Exodus 19:8, we read, 'The people all responded together, "We will do everything the LORD has said"' (see also Exodus 24:3-7). As Jonathan Sacks puts it, a free God seeks the free worship of free human beings.

The Book of Exodus is an example of God intervening directly in history on behalf of the poor and oppressed and forming them into a nation.

---

or%20the%20sabbath%E2%80%9D.
More examples can be found on Wikipedia
https://en.wikipedia.org/wiki/Chiastic_structure

According to Maimonides (Jewish scholar, 11th c.) **'What is primary in Exodus is not the miracles, but monotheism'**, the idea of a single God whose sovereignty extends everywhere – hence the plagues in Egypt.[11] Every people has its own god, but the God of Israel shows that he can act in Egypt, in a foreign country protected by its own gods, for example by provoking plagues. He is the universal God. This is the primary message of Exodus.

3) The subtext: God (and Moses) as educator

According to Jonathan Sacks, Exodus has not only a surface text, God as liberator, but a sub-text, God as educator. For this reason, many episodes in Exodus are related twice (see the table below), first as a miraculous action by God alone and a second time as an action undertaken by the people together with God.

This interpretation of the book of Exodus is a radically different interpretation from Julius Wellhausen's 'documentary hypothesis' (1878), with its four sources Jahwist (J), Elohist (E), Deuteronomist (D), and Priestly (P). Readers familiar with this source criticism of the OT must put it to the back of their minds if they are to learn from the classical interpretations of Rabbinic Judaism which Jonathan Sacks expounds.

In Jonathan Sacks's interpretation, first the Israelites experience a miracle, such as God making the two tablets on Mount Horeb, but this does not change them. Then the episode of the Golden Calf

---

[11] Rambam, Mishneh Torah, Yesodei HaTorah 8:1

follows and the tablets are smashed. Moses returns to the mountain, but this time Moses hands God the tablets which he has made himself and on which God writes a second time (Exodus 34:1-4).

Before the episode of the Golden Calf, the Israelites miraculously receive God's instructions about making the sanctuary, but do nothing about it. After the episode of the Golden Calf, the Israelites make the sanctuary together, following God's instructions (see table below). **It is not seeing miracles, but doing something together that changes the Israelites.**

The table below lists examples of this repeat pattern in the book of Exodus.

The power of God and the passivity of man (dependency)	The will of God internalised by man (inter-dependency)
Battle before crossing the 'sea of reeds' against Pharoah and his chariots (14:9-31)[12]	Battle immediately after against the Amalekites, (17:8-16)
First set of stone tablets, prepared and written by God. Then the Golden Calf, broken by Moses	Later second set of stone tablets, Moses prepares the tablets, God writes them

[12] For the term, 'sea of reeds' see; https://en.wikipedia.org/wiki/Yam_Suph#:~:text=More%2Orecently%2C%20alt ernative%20understandings%20of,than%20as%20'Red%20Sea'.

God in a cloud of Glory at Sinai (24:15-18)	God in a cloud of Glory in the tabernacle, built by the Israelites (40:34-35)
The Sinai covenant declared by God (20:1-14)	A second time by Moses, reading from the 'book of the covenant' which he had written (24:1-11)
God's instructions about the construction of the tabernacle before the Golden Calf (25–30)	And after (35-40), how the people carried out God's instructions

Where man repeats the action with God's help, having internalised God's intentions, this is not some form of Pelagianism, of human beings becoming virtuous in their own strength, but about acting with God. To quote Nicholas Henshall (recently the Dean of Chelmsford Anglican cathedral), 'In the first place [virtues] are God's gift to us and in the second place we need to respond, to embed them in our lives – actively practicing love, joy, peace, forbearance, kindness, goodness, faithfulness, gentleness and self-control.' Paul makes the same point in Romans 5:4, 'We also rejoice in our sufferings, because we know that suffering produces perseverance; perseverance, character; and character, hope.' It is by acting out the virtues that character is forged, that we develop virtuous habits and that we become virtuous.[13] But it is God who both shows us the goal and gives us the strength to persevere. A footnote in the Jerusalem Bible reads, 'A typical example of Pauline moral teaching: become what you are already. Do in your lives what Christ did in you when you became Christians.'

4) Israel as a signal of transcendence

Israel is called to be a signal of transcendence. As we read in Deuteronomy, 'The LORD did not set his affection on you and choose you because you were more numerous than other peoples, for you were the fewest of all peoples.' (Deuteronomy 7:7). The survival and success of Israel, such a weak and small nation, was in the ancient world and is today a signal that the Israelites' success came not from their own strength, but the powerful help of God. In the same way, in Genesis, God always chooses the younger son. In 1 Cor. 1:27 Paul writes, 'God chose the weak things of the world to shame the strong.' As Jonathan Sacks concludes, 'The Jewish people, its laws, its way of life, continually testifies to something greater than itself.'[14]

---

[13] This is also the essence of Aristotle's 'Virtue Ethics' which have been revived in the twentieth century by Alasdair MacIntyre and others.
[14] Jonathan Sacks, Commentary on Exodus, introduction (adapted).

5) Six compassionate and courageous women in Exodus

Jonathan Sacks points out that Exodus is not just about men. It also contains the portraits of six compassionate women. Yocheved, Moses's mother, has the courage to have a child when she knows that Pharaoh has ordered that all newborn male children be killed. Then Miriam, Moses's sister speaks to Pharaoh's daughter who has recently discovered baby Moses in the reeds. Miriam cunningly arranges for Yocheved, Moses's real biological mother, to be Moses's milk nurse. This same Miriam later has a major role in the Exodus story.

The two midwives, Shifrah and Puah, defy Pharaoh's genocidal decree. They save the life of Moses and doubtless other Jewish baby boys. We are never told if these two midwives are or are not Jewish themselves. When Moses has grown up, his Midianite wife, Zipporah, saves his life (Exodus 4:25). Finally, most startling of all, Pharaoh's daughter rescues Moses and adopts him, even though she is acting in contravention of her father's will, of the will of Pharaoh, the absolute ruler of the land.

Exercise 1 – How can Exodus help us interpret the New Testament?

Participants in the course are invited to come up with any suggestions.

The application of the Torah to the NT, an overview

The Christian Bible has two main story arcs;

a) A (mainly) political liberation (the book of Exodus). Moses liberates the Hebrew slaves and builds them into a nation.

b) A spiritual liberation (the NT). By his cross and resurrection, Christ frees us from enslavement to sin and leaves us the Holy Spirit to guide us into the full truth and into the Kingdom. (Christ ... rescues us from the present evil age. Galatians 1:4). Note that in 1 Corinthians 10, Paul specifically applies the book of Exodus to the Christian life.

6) How does the book of Exodus help us understand the NT?

Seeing that the Hebrew scriptures, and the Torah in particular, were probably the only text the gospel writers knew, and that they knew it well, it is to be expected that both its structures and its themes are echoed in the New Testament.

A. How the structure of Exodus helps us understand the NT

In Matthew, the Beatitudes are 'the new law' delivered in the 'sermon on the mount' by 'the new Moses' who does not abolish but fulfils the law (Matthew 5:3-10). Note that both the Beatitudes and the Ten Commandments are written so as to be memorised.[15]

---

[15] Gervase Vernon. The countenance of Christ: A commentary on the

The main body of Matthew's gospel has often been seen as a 'mini-Torah' of five books.[16]

The next interpretation I offer with great hesitation as it is no more than a suggestion. If we consider Luke-Acts as one book, then we can see a chiastic structure. The crucifixion/resurrection/ascension narrative is in the middle. The 'passion of Paul' in Acts 13-28 mirrors that of Jesus in Luke.[17]

Luke/Acts begins by promising to give an account to Theophilus of 'the things that have been fulfilled among us' (Luke 1:1). Luke is going to describe, in his two books, the fulfilment of the Torah, of the promises in the Torah. Luke states that he will give 'an ordered account' (Luke 1:3). But by this, does he mean an account with the chiastic structures seen in the Torah? Or does he mean the logical sequential account that we now think of as an ordered account?

For Luke, Pentecost in Acts is a 'new giving of the Ten commandments'. Philo (Jewish scholar, 25 BCE to 50 CE), describes Pentecost as the feast of the giving of the Law.[18] In Acts, at Pentecost, the apostles proclaim how Jesus fulfils Israel's scriptures. Because Luke places this giving of the new ten commandments at Pentecost, he cannot have a 'sermon on the

---

Beatitudes in Matthew. Independently published, 2022.

[16] Raymond Brown. Introduction to the New Testament. Doubleday, 1997. Chapter 8, p.172.

[17] Carlo Maria Martini, The Gospel According to St. Paul: Meditations on His Life and Letters. Word Among Us, 2008.

[18] Philo, 'De Decalogo' Chapter 11:44-49
http://www.earlyjewishwritings.com/text/philo/book26.html

mount', a new ten commandments, in the middle of his gospel as Matthew does, but has instead his 'sermon on the plain' (Luke 6:20-49).

Luke – Acts. A proposed chiastic structure

	Place	Chapter
A	Galilee	Luke 4:14–9:50
B	The journey to Jerusalem through Judea and Samaria	Luke 9:51–19:40
C	Jerusalem, the passion	Luke 19:41–24:49
D	Ascension/Pentecost, the giving of the new Ten Commandments	Luke 24:50–Acts 2
C	Jerusalem	Acts 1:12–8:1a
B	Judea and Samaria	Acts 8:1b–11:18
A	To the ends of the earth	Acts 11:19–28:31

Adapted from K. R. Wolfe, "The Chiastic Structure of Luke-Acts and Some Implications for Worship," Southwestern Journal of Theology 22 (1980): 67. See at:
https://www.chiasmusxchange.com/

B. How the themes of Exodus help us understand the NT

Here I can do no more than hint at a vast subject. One of the main themes found in Exodus by Jonathan Sacks is, 'God as educator'.

Consider the miracle of the loaves. Jesus does not simply produce bread out of nothing, but chooses to use the few loaves brought voluntarily by the crowd, then gets the disciples to hand them out, thus acting as both miracle maker and educator.

Consider the evil spirit who is cleansed. If we do nothing, the evil spirit comes back with seven friends (Matthew 12:45). After a miraculous cleansing, we must furnish our souls with new habits, or we will fall back into our old ways.

The other main theme is God as liberator. Christ is the new Moses who frees us from Satan and death and overcomes them.[19] In Mark and the other synoptic gospels, Jesus is often depicted as having power over demons, and freeing people from their demons.

7   The sanctuary as a type of Christ

The emphasis in the second half of the book of Exodus is on plans to build a portable but empty tabernacle instead of making an idol such as the Golden Calf,. This tabernacle the Israelites carried with them and it was a place where God could be especially present. Later, the inner sanctuary of the temple replaced the tabernacle and was also empty. The emptiness of the tabernacle and the temple sanctuary signified that no idol was worshipped. It also signified a God who is beyond human conception or understanding. However, he is a God who reveals Himself, who chooses to communicate with his people not only in deeds but also in words which they can

---

[19] Bryan D. Estelle. Echoes of Exodus: Tracing a Biblical Motif. 2018.

understand. The tabernacle and, later, the inner sanctuary of the temple contained the words of the ten commandments engraved on two tablets, words which God had revealed to his people.

Many people have seen the sanctuary as a type,[20] as a foreshadowing of Christ.[21] He is 'greater than the Temple' (Matthew 12:7). Christ is the place where God is on earth, as the empty sanctuary and later the temple had been the place where God was especially present. If we want to follow Christ, we have to empty ourselves, just as the tabernacle was empty. 'How blessed are the poor in spirit, the kingdom of Heaven is theirs' (Mt. 5:3). I love the parallel saying of the Baal Shem Tov (Jewish 18th-century founder of Hasidism), 'Those who are full of themselves, have no room left for God.' [22]

After the destruction of the second temple and its sanctuary in AD 70, Jewish communities needed a new focus for unity. For the writer of the letter to the Hebrews, this new focus is provided by the 'Heavenly sanctuary' to which Christians have access through Jesus. For many Jews, God's presence, the Shekinah, went into exile with them.[23]

---

[20] For type and antitype see; https://en.wikipedia.org/wiki/Typology_(theology)
[21] For a detailed and convincing run through of the analogies between Christ and the sanctuary/tabernacle see; https://bcf-church.org/wp-content/uploads/2018/01/Jesus-and-the-Tabernacle.pdf
[22] https://www.azquotes.com/quote/714292. Probably from Martin Buber. The legend of the Baal-Shem. T&T Clark, 1955.
[23] See the Jewish Encyclopaedia; https://www.jewishencyclopedia.com/articles/13537-shekinah

A summary of Exodus: Becoming what we are

This is Sack's interpretation of the book of Exodus. God miraculously delivers a people, but then he laboriously leads them to become a nation; to internalise what he has already made them by giving them tasks to do together.

In a similar vein Martin Luther King wrote '[God] is seeking at every moment of His existence to lift men from the bondage of some evil Egypt, carrying them through the wilderness of discipline, and finally to the promised land of personal and social integration.'[24]

This is also the Jerusalem bible's summary of Paul's teaching in the footnote quoted above. Or in a similar mode, Paul in Romans

---

'Wheresoever the Israelites went in exile the Shekinah accompanied them; and when they were redeemed it likewise was released' (Meg. 29a; see also R. H. 3a; B. Ķ. 25a; Zeb. 118b; Soṭah 5a; Shab. 67a).

'For other Jews, 'the flesh became word'. In other words, temple worship with its many sacrifices (flesh) was replaced by prayer, synagogues and scripture study (word).' Jesper Svartvik. *Reconciliation and Transformation: Reconsidering Christian Theologies of the Cross*. Cascade books, 2021.For yet other Jews, temple worship was merely suspended.

A further Jewish response to the fall of the Temple is reported in a conversation between Rabbi Jochanan ben Zaqqai and his disciple Rabbi Jehoshua (Avot de-Rabbi Natan 4.5). God wants mercy, not sacrifice (Hosea 6:6). Though the temple sacrifices no longer occur, acts of good will can reconcile the sins of the people.

In summary, there were a variety of Jewish responses to the fall of the temple, as there were a variety of Christian responses. Japer Svartvik. Op. cit.

[24] From the rousing final lines of Martin Luther King's sermon 'The death of evil on the seashore.'

https://kinginstitute.stanford.edu/king-papers/documents/draft-chapter-viii-death-evil-upon-seashore

5:1-5 starts with a classic declaration of justification by faith, but immediately follows with a description of how suffering builds character. (See also Ephesians 2:1-8.)

Questions to consider as a larger group

1) Exodus is about 'the liberation of the poor and oppressed'. **How is our church community involved in such work?**

2) God, through Moses, did not just liberate the oppressed, but formed them into a nation. He formed them into a nation by living with them and by giving them tasks to do together, tasks to which all could contribute. **What tasks is our church community 'doing together' so that we can become in reality the community we already are 'in Christ'?**

3) How can your church become a **'signal of transcendence'?**

4) Christ as the antitype of the empty sanctuary (as him whom the sanctuary foreshadows). **How can we empty ourselves, so that God may be present in us?**

Further Questions to consider in small groups, if time allows

1) Each in turn, in your groups, describe what your church is currently doing.

2) Then, each in turn, set out your hopes for what your church might do.

3) Ask yourselves how this Jewish reading of the book of Exodus has altered the way in which you think about your church, where it is going and how it might get there.

4. WEEK 3. BOBOWA AND THE SHOAH

Week 3 should be led by a member of the Jewish community talking about the Holocaust and other topics, such as the state of Israel, he considers important for today. However, if nobody can be found to give such a talk, the following article, about the Holocaust (also known as the Shoah) can be used instead. It is a microhistory focused on the tiny village of Bobowa from which my mother came.

Bobowa and the Shoah

1. Bobowa

Bobowa (Bobov in Yiddish) was the village in the foothills of the Tatra mountains where my mother went for her summer holidays. Bobowa was a small place, consisting of something like 700 Jewish Poles living round the market place and another 700 Christian Poles in the rest of the village. She and her family went there because her uncle Kazimierz Wieniawa Długoszowski

(Kazek) lived in the manor house. After his mother's death in 1924, Kazek was the squire of Bobowa. The photograph below is of Kazek, wearing military uniform, and Rabbi Halberstam (the Chasidic rabbi of Bobowa (Bobov)) taken in 1939 just before the war.[25] The purpose of the photograph was to encourage the rabbi's many followers to buy Polish government bonds and support the Polish army in the imminent fight with Germany.

Kazek and Rabbi Ben Zion Halberstam in 1939, just before the outbreak of the war.

---

[25] From: *Jewish society in Poland*. Skotnicki, Aleksander and Klimczak, Wladyslaw. Wydawnictwo AA, 2009.
ISBN 10 8361060766, ISBN 13 9788361060765

During the war, Kazek acted as the mayor of Bobowa. Very likely German soldiers were billeted in the manor house and he had to live elsewhere. Much of the village was turned into a concentration village and Jews from the surrounding farms and villages were herded behind barbed wire. Poles were not allowed in this area and Kazek probably had nothing to do with its administration.

At some point during the war, Kazek furnished false papers to a Jewish tailor from Tarnow. This man managed to escape to Israel where he must have told his story. Alas, the Nazis eventually took (almost) all the Jews from the "concentration village" and killed them in Garbacz forest not far away in the direction of the Tatra mountains[26].

In 1971, when I first visited, Bobowa gave an impression of grinding poverty; agriculture still depended on horses working tiny strips of land. The market square was simply earth. The synagogue was locked, but somebody was maintaining the Jewish cemetery. Today, in 2023, Bobowa is a thriving village, largely rebuilt and not dissimilar to a prosperous village in a tourist area of Britain. The synagogue has been returned to Jewish ownership and restored. It can be visited, but the Jewish cemetery, also returned to Jewish ownership, is now fenced in and locked.

---

[26] *Restless memories, recollections of the Holocaust years*, Samuel P. Oliner, Judah L. Magnes Museum, Berkeley, California.

2. The progress of our knowledge about the Garbacz graves

When I visited the village of Bobowa in southern Poland in August 1971, my cousin Ala, then a mother with two teenage children, was living in a small house in the woods nearby. She had lived there during the war when she would have been a young woman. None of the Jews of Bobowa had survived the war, as far as she knew; she believed that the Jews in Bobowa had been killed in Auschwitz. Bobowa is on a train line to Tarnów; Auschwitz seemed the obvious place. She told me that she had personally witnessed Germans driving through the ghetto of Bobowa and "shooting the Jews like rabbits".

In 1979 Professor Samuel Oliner published the first edition of his reminiscences; *Restless Memories, Recollections of the Holocaust Years*.[27] In this he revealed that the Jews of the "concentration ghetto" in Bobowa, when the ghetto was liquidated, were taken to a wood, about half an hour away, called "Garbacz" and shot there. He had been living in the ghetto as a young boy but managed to hide and escape during the final liquidation. Therefore, he was not present at the executions and did not witness them. After the war, in 1945, he returned to Bobowa and, with others, built a concrete memorial at the site of the shooting in Garbacz forest. Not originally from Bobowa, he was taken there in June 1942 during

---

[27] *Restless memories, recollections of the Holocaust years*, Samuel P. Oliner, Judah L. Magnes Museum, Berkeley, California.

the war when it had become a concentration ghetto for Jews from the local area. After the war, he was unable to stay in Poland due to anti-Semitic incidents and emigrated to America where he became a professor of sociology. He spent a lifetime studying "the altruistic personality"; people like the Polish peasant woman, Balwina, who had saved his life after he escaped from the ghetto. When Professor Oliner returned in 1982 to the Garbacz site he met a witness of the massacre.[28]

In the 2000s Fr Patrick Desbois started his "Shoah par balles" (Holocaust by bullets) project, unearthing the mass graves left by the Einsatzgruppen, the SS death squads tasked with killing Jews in the areas of Eastern Europe occupied by the German army. On the map on his "Yahad-In Unum" website[29], the nearest site of mass killing to Bobowa is the village of Stróżówka. If you look up this locality on his website you find that:

"At the beginning of 1940, the Nazis created a ghetto in Bobowa. In October 1941, a ghetto was established in the nearby town, Gorlice. Jews from Gorlice and neighbouring villages were all gathered there. Deportations to the death camp, Bełżec, and mass executions started in the spring of 1942. On August 14, 1942, several trucks filled with Jews arrived in Stróżówka from the Gorlice and Bobowa ghettos. All these Jews, about 700 old and

---

[28] P 176–177 in *Narrow Escapes* Samuel Oliner 2000 Paragon House, St Paul, Minnesota. This is a later version of his book *Restless Memories* mentioned above.
[29] http://www.yahadinunum.org/

sick people, were shot on the so-called presbytery square and in the Garbacz forest near Stróżówka. According to Wladyslawa Z., born in 1928, an eyewitness quoted on the website, the Germans were waiting near the cemetery for all the trucks to arrive. The Jews from Gorlice were already shortlisted. The selection of others took place near the road. Elderly people were put aside. Young people were still useful. The Jews were led to the pit by young Polish men from Baudienst[30] (Polish labour battalion) whom the Nazis forced to drink alcohol and [then] help them during the execution process."

This information is now present in precis form on the English version of Wikipedia, though not the French or the Russian versions. It is also on Polish Wikipedia[31], with a photo of the memorial in Garbacz forest.

---

[30] "Baudienst was the Polish labour battalion created by Nazi Germany in the "Generalgouvernement" territory of occupied Poland.

[31]

https://pl.wikipedia.org/wiki/Cmentarz_%C5%BCydowski_w_Str%C3%B3%C5%BC%C3%B3wce

After the war, the memorial was erected in Garbacz forest. The inscription, translated into English, reads, 'In this mass grave / rest nearly 1000 jews / from Gorlice and Bobowa: / victims of hitlerian beastly slaughter / on august 14, 1942. / The erection of this monument / on this holy ground / was done by Nachum Ormanier / and Jakub Peller, the chairman of the/ county Jewish committee of Gorlice.'[32]

Looking back, I see this as the story of the gradual emergence of knowledge about these terrible crimes against humanity, hidden for so long. It is also a warning, as Fr Desbois says, to other "would be mass murderers", that crimes like these cannot be hidden for ever,

---

[32] Photo from:
https://pl.wikipedia.org/wiki/Cmentarz_%C5%BCydowski_w_Str%C3%B3%5%BC%C3%B3wce

that "your brother's blood will cry out to me from the ground," as the Bible has it (Genesis 4,10).

3. The search for Eliezer Unger

At the outbreak of the war, my Great-Uncle Kazek was the squire of the village of Bobowa in Southern Poland. During the war he would have had little to do with the Jews of Bobowa whom the Nazis soon enclosed in a ghetto in the centre of the village. The ghetto had its own governing council, the Judenrat, whose leader was Mr. Messenger.

Most of the Jews of Bobowa belonged to a very devout and influential Chassidic community led by Rabbi Ben Zion Halberstam.[33] As the war progressed, this ghetto was used by the Nazis to house Jews evicted from nearby farms and villages. As more Jews arrived, others were sent to forced-labour camps or were killed, and as a result, the numbers in the Bobowa ghetto fluctuated. In August 1942, all the survivors, about 700 of them, were taken in lorries to the Garbacz forest further into the Tatra mountains, and most were shot and killed.[34] This was part of the first phase of the Holocaust, or Shoah, called the 'Holocaust by bullets'. Less well known than the later industrialised mass murder of the extermination and concentration camps, the 'Holocaust by

---

[33] Rabbi Ben Zion Halberstam (1874 – 1941)
[34] „Boże iskry". Synagoga w Bobowej. A very accurate history of the Jews of Bobowa from earliest times, including WW II
https://www.youtube.com/watch?v=XiSIyHXZuOE

bullets' was responsible for approximately 1.5 million deaths.[35] The later second phase, the industrialised murder, led to 2.7 million deaths, while 1.8 million Jews died from hunger and disease, adding up to the widely accepted total of six million deaths of Jews in World War II.[36] I shall come back to this number of 6 million. The third phase, the killing of those Jews in hiding, the 'Hunt for the Jews', or Judenjagd, added little to the total number of Jews killed.

There were a small number of Jewish survivors from pre-war Bobowa, most of whom had escaped before the final liquidation. Some returned to Bobowa after the war and erected a monument to the dead at the site of the execution in Garbacz forest.[37]

Sadly, they found themselves unwelcome in post-war Poland, now ruled by a communist government. Many made their way to Israel. Here, after the war, the Jewish survivors of Bobowa, as did those

---

[35] https://en.wikipedia.org/wiki/Holocaust_by_Bullets
[36] https://en.wikipedia.org/wiki/Extermination_camp
[37] Other survivors among the pre-war Jewish inhabitants of Bobowa are documented. A number of members of the Halberstam family (the family of the rabbi) escaped before the final destruction. They settled in New York after the war and founded a new Bobover community which has flourished. Their odyssey is recorded in
Devorah Gliksman. *Nor the moon by night*. Feldheim publishers, New York and Jerusalem, 1997.
Two other boys, besides Professor Oliner, escaped the destruction of the ghetto. Their details are in,
Sir Martin Gilbert. *The Boys: Triumph Over Adversity*. Phoenix, 2003.

of many other Jewish Polish communities, wrote a Yizkor or memorial book. [38]

Unusually for one of these Yizkor books, the Polish mayor of the village, my Great Uncle Kazek, receives a positive mention. He is credited with avoiding epidemics in the ghetto and saving the life of a man from Tarnów, the son of a rabbi Unger. Kazek, it is written, saved Mr. Unger by giving him false papers. (Tarnów is the nearest big town to Bobowa, about an hour's distance on a single-track branch line which had been built by Kazek's father.)

For many years I searched for this survivor named 'Unger', but without success. For Kazek to have been named and catalogued at Yad Vashem as 'righteous among the nations' it would have been necessary for Mr. Unger to deposit a sworn testimony at Yad Vashem. This he clearly did not do. Kazek himself, in all likelihood, never spoke about his war time action, about issuing false papers to save a life. It would have been suicidal to do this

---

[38] https://www.jewishgen.org/yizkor/pinkas_poland/pol3_00063.html
Encyclopaedia of Jewish Communities, Poland (Volume III) Western Galicia • Silesia
Translation of Pinkas hakehillot Polin: entsiklopedyah shel ha-yishuvim ha-Yehudiyim
le-min hivasdam ve-`ad le-ahar Sho'at Milhemet ha-`olam ha-sheniyah.
Edited by: Abraham Wein & Aharon Weiss
Authors: Zvi Avital, Danuta Dabrowska, Smuel Levin, Yitzhak Mais, Wila Orbach, Abraham Wein, Aharon Weiss
Published by Yad Vashem. Yad Vashem, Jerusalem 1984, 399 pages, Hebrew.
Pages 63–64

while the Nazis were in Poland and such actions were not much better received in post-war Bobowa.

Looking again this year, now that so much more material is online, I have found a possible candidate, who may be the man whom Kazek saved. These days both the Tarnów and Bobowa Yizkor books are online, and Yad Vashem provides long, but necessarily incomplete lists of those living in Bobowa and Tarnów during the war, and of their fates. To read these lists on the Yad Vashem website is a singularly depressing experience since almost all the Jews are recorded as murdered. Of the few, well under 10% who survived, the commonest reason for survival is that they managed to reach the Soviet Union during the Soviet – Nazi partition of Poland in 1939, a partition made in accordance with the Molotov–Ribbentrop Pact.[39]

The list of Jews from Tarnów at Yad Vashem shows that there was at least one rabbi Eliezer Unger there who died in the Shoah, but he had no surviving sons according to that list.[40] Unger was anyway a common Jewish name in Tarnów and throughout the region. The record at Yad Vashem of survivors from Tarnów

---

[39] https://en.wikipedia.org/wiki/Molotov%E2%80%93Ribbentrop_Pact
[40]https://yvng.yadvashem.org/index.html?language=en&s_id=&s_lastName=Ungar&s_firstName=&s_place=Tarnów&s_dateOfBirth=&cluster=true
He is also mentioned in the Tarnów Yizkor book,
https://www.jewishgen.org/yizkor/Tarnów/tar2_219.html
However, only one daughter is recorded as surviving. He appears at the Geni.com website;
https://www.geni.com/people/R-Eleazar-Unger-Admur-Jabna-Tarmow/6000000007727242463

named Unger shows eight survivors out of 88 records of people of that name (78 of the other Ungers are recorded as murdered). There is no record of somebody whose survival account matches the story given in the Bobowa Yizkor book.[41] One survivor from Tarnów, who appears in the Yad Vashem archive, Israel Unger, did write his story and published it as 'The untold diary of Israel Unger'. He is clearly the wrong Unger as he hid with his family in a secret compartment in a flour mill in Tarnów throughout the war.[42] His account forms a contrast with the better-known *Diary of Anne Frank*. His family's hiding place was far more primitive than that of the Frank family, but, unlike the Franks, his family was not denounced. Although it is likely that many of the mill's workers were aware of the presence of a Jewish family hidden in the mill, they survived the war and nobody denounced them. Few Jews in hiding in Poland survived this third part of the Holocaust, the 'Hunt for the Jews', or Judenjagd. This name, the 'Hunt for the Jews', was no metaphor. There are many reports of Nazis engaged in the hunt wearing traditional hunting clothes. I myself have heard an eyewitness, my cousin Ala Olejniczak, describe how Nazis drove through the Bobowa ghetto 'shooting the Jews as you might shoot rabbits'. While numerically responsible for a very small

---

[41]https://yvng.yadvashem.org/index.html?language=en&s_id=&s_lastName=Unger&s_firstName=&s_place=Tarnów&s_dateOfBirth=&cluster=true
[42] https://www.amazon.co.uk/Unwritten-Diary-Israel-Unger-Writing/dp/1771120118/ref=tmm_pap_swatch_0?_encoding=UTF8&qid=&sr=
Carolyn Gammon. *The Unwritten Diary of Israel Unger*. Wilfrid Laurier University Press, 2014.

proportion of total Jewish deaths, this Judenjagd has scarred Polish – Jewish relations more than the first two phases of the Shoah. Poles who were hiding Jews were faced with the impossible choice of likely death for themselves and their families, or the betrayal and killing of the Jews they had sheltered.

One possible candidate for the man saved by my great uncle is someone named Eliezer Unger. As I mentioned above, an Eliezer Unger is described in the Tarnów Yizkor book as having written down his memories of the event and his account is extensively quoted in that book. His name does not appear in the Yad Vashem records for Tarnów, but these records are incomplete.

An internet search for the name 'Eliezer Unger' leads to an article in 'The Jerusalem Post' in 2020 entitled, 'Who came up with the number of Jews murdered in the Holocaust?'[43] The article is about Eliezer Unger. It does not state that he came from Tarnów, but only that he was a leader of a religious Zionist movement, HaShomer HaDati. This Eliezer Unger escapes rather late from the terrors of the Shoah (1943–1944) and manages to get out of Poland via Slovakia, which is just South of Bobowa, and then through Hungary to Israel. He must have needed false papers to make that

---

[43] https://www.jpost.com/jerusalem-report/who-came-up-with-the-number-of-jews-murdered-in-the-Shoah-625678
The Jerusalem Post. Article, 'Who came up with the number of Jews murdered in the Shoah?' By Joel Rappel Published: MAY 7, 2020 19:31
The writer works at the Institute for Shoah Studies, Bar-Ilan University and established and runs the Elie Wiesel Archive at Boston University.

escape. Did he get them from my Great-Uncle Kazek? In Israel, he is documented as the first person to use the number of '6 million' as the number of Jews killed during the Shoah. Since, in 1944, the war was still ongoing, this is clearly not a claim to have counted the dead. Rather the figure '6 million' was then widely accepted as the number of Jews in Europe. What Eliezer was claiming was that almost all the Jews in Europe had been killed. In this, alas, history proved him to have been substantially correct. [44]

From the moment he arrived in Palestine in 1944, which was while the war was still continuing and the horrors of the Shoah were not yet widely known, he made it his work to publicize the Shoah among the Jewish communities of Palestine. In the Jerusalem Post article we read, 'Ungar would go from one synagogue to another, walk up to the central platform – with or without permission – and yell and scream on behalf of the Jews who still remained alive in Europe. He went to dozens of religious Zionist synagogues, most of the members did not want to hear him, and he was often thrown out.' People, in other words, did not want to hear his message about the massacres happening in Europe. A similar reluctance to hear and believe their message was met by other witness survivors who made it to the UK and the USA, such as Jan Karski.[45] In 1947,

---

[44] https://www.haaretz.com/israel-news/2020-04-21/ty-article/.premium/figure-of-6-million-Shoah-victims-first-cited-by-polish-survivor-not-eichmann/0000017f-f276-d487-abff-f3fec7930000
[45] https://en.wikipedia.org/wiki/Jan_Karski

Eliezer left Israel in despair. He resurfaced later as a Jewish teacher in Uruguay.[46]

This Eliezer Unger would likely have been in Jerusalem at the time the Bobowa Yizkor book was being compiled and may be the source of the information about the rescue of one Jew from Tarnów by Kazek. Indeed he may have been that Jew.

List of resources on the Holocaust in Bobowa

Books

1) Samuel P. Oliner. *Restless memories, recollections of the Holocaust years*. Judah L. Magnes Museum, Berkeley, California, 1986.

2) Samuel Oliner. *Narrow Escapes*. Paragon House, St Paul, Minnesota, 2000. (This is a later edition of the former book)

3) *Jewish society in Poland*. Skotnicki, Aleksander and Klimczak, Wladyslaw. Wydawnictwo AA, 2009.

4) Devorah Gliksman. *Nor the moon by night*. Feldheim publishers, New York and Jerusalem, 1997. (this describes the escape of members of Rabbi Halberstam's family)

---

[46] https://www.jpost.com/jerusalem-report/who-came-up-with-the-number-of-jews-murdered-in-the-Shoah-625678

5) Sir Martin Gilbert. *The Boys: Triumph Over Adversity.* Phoenix, 2003. (mentions two other survivors of the Bobowa ghetto).

6) Carolyn Gammon. *The Unwritten Diary of Israel Unger.* Wilfrid Laurier University Press, 2014. (the story of a survivor from Tarnow)

7) The Bobowa Yizkor or memorial book is in; *Encyclopaedia of Jewish Communities, Poland (Volume III)* Western Galicia • Silesia. Translation of Pinkas hakehillot Polin: entsiklopedyah shel ha-yishuvim ha-Yehudiyim le-min hivasdam ve-`ad le-ahar Sho'at Milhemet ha-`olam ha-sheniyah. Edited by: Abraham Wein & Aharon Weiss. Authors: Zvi Avital, Danuta Dabrowska, Smuel Levin, Yitzhak Mais, Wila Orbach, Abraham Wein, Aharon Weiss. Published by Yad Vashem. Yad Vashem, Jerusalem 1984, 399 pages, Hebrew. Pages 63-64 https://www.jewishgen.org/yizkor/pinkas_poland/pol3_000 63.html

8) The Tarnów Yizkor book, https://www.jewishgen.org/yizkor/Tarnów/tar2_219.html

Websites

1) The website of Fr Desbois's "Shoah par balles" (Holocaust by bullets) project
http://www.yahadinunum.org/

2) Polish Wikipedia entry for Jewish cemetery in Stróżówka;

https://pl.wikipedia.org/wiki/Cmentarz_%C5%BCydowski_w_Str%C3%B3%C5%BC%C3%B3wce

3) English Wikipedia entries on the Holocaust

https://en.wikipedia.org/wiki/Holocaust_by_Bullets

https://en.wikipedia.org/wiki/Extermination_camp

4) Yad Vashem database of survivors from Tarnow

https://yvng.yadvashem.org/index.html?language=en&s_id=&s_lastName=Ungar&s_firstName=&s_place=Tarnów&s_dateOfBirth=&cluster=true

YouTube Video

„Boże iskry". Synagoga w Bobowej. A very accurate history of the Jews of Bobowa from earliest times, including WW II

https://www.youtube.com/watch?v=XiSIyHXZu0E

Newspaper article

The Jerusalem Post. 'Who came up with the number of Jews murdered in the Shoah?' Joel Rappel. May 7, 2020.

https://www.jpost.com/jerusalem-report/who-came-up-with-the-number-of-jews-murdered-in-the-Shoah-625678

5. Week 4. The Holocaust and Christian anti-Judaism

There is no change of mind on God's part about the gifts he has made or of his choice. (Romans 11:29).

An essay written as a personal response to Rabbi Jonathan Sacks's book 'Not in God's Name: Confronting Religious Violence' (1)

Introduction

For the German Roman Catholic theologian Johann Baptist Metz, or the Jewish philosopher Rabbi Emil Fackenheim, the Holocaust, known to Jews as the Shoah, was the only theological problem for the twentieth century. Now, in the twenty-first century, others may see it as just one of a number of genocides in recent history. But for somebody like myself, whose half-Jewish mother came from a Polish village where almost all the Jews were killed during the Holocaust, it remains the defining problem.

The Holocaust was motivated by the anti-Semitism of a non-Christian group, the Nazis. Anti-Semitism is prejudice against

Jews on account of their race. Anti-Judaism, on the other hand, is prejudice against Jews on account of their religion. Christian anti-Judaism, alas, was one of the roots of modern anti-Semitism in the West. At the very least, as Pope John Paul II said, it lulled the conscience of some Christians so that they did not respond to anti-Semitism as vigorously as they should have done (18). I would put it more strongly. As Rabbi Jonathan Sacks said when he addressed the Lambeth conference in 2008, for the last one thousand years, to Jews the word 'Christian' has meant fear; has meant inquisition, exclusion, expulsion and so on.[47] Why study Christian anti-Judaism during Lent? Because, in many lands and at many times, Easter week has been a week of fear for Jewish communities, a week in which they retreated to their homes for fear of violent Christian mobs. Clearly, Christians have, at times, so misunderstood Easter week as to allow it to lead them to hatred rather than love. We need to re-examine our reading of the scriptures to ensure this does not happen again.

In this essay I am presenting for a Christian audience just a few passages from the long history of Christian anti-Judaism.[48] In Ephesians, Paul wrote that Jesus had broken down the wall of

---

[47] The video of Jonathan Sacks addressing the 2008 Lambeth conference is at; https://www.rabbisacks.org/videos/faith-and-fate-the-lambeth-conference-address/

[48] For many of the details in this essay I am indebted to Rabbi Jonathan Sacks's wonderful book, *Not in God's Name: Confronting Religious Violence* (1). Rabbi Jonathan Sacks (1948-2020) was Chief Rabbi of the Orthodox synagogues in the UK. My essay is by no means a full discussion of the topic. An authoritative account is in Edward Kessler, *An introduction to Jewish-Christian relations* (2).

hostility between Jews and Gentiles (Ephesians 2:14). He was referring to an eternal reality accomplished by Christ on the cross, but not yet fully realised on earth.[49] Sadly, since Paul wrote those words, Jews and Christians have largely chosen to stay safely within their own group without crossing over the now destroyed wall. It is only since the Holocaust shocked both Jews and gentiles to the core that some brave but tentative steps towards reconciliation have been taken on both sides. It is these steps that I want to celebrate here, having first sketched the background.

In the first decades after the resurrection of Jesus, there was no clear distinction between the followers of the new Way and the Jewish religion. Christians were initially seen by themselves and others as a Jewish sect. In this period before the fall of the second temple, disputes within Judaism, for example between Sadducees and Pharisees, reached a pitch of intensity that had not been seen before. As the historian Josephus attests, the peak of this ferocity was reached in the communal strife during the siege of Jerusalem and contributed to the final destruction of the city by the Romans in 70 CE. Some of the rhetoric in early Christian documents must be understood against this background. Internecine strife within one group can lead to more vicious rhetoric than arguments between groups, just as civil wars can be the most violent of wars.

---

[49] Some commentators read this passage as not referring to a change in an 'eternal reality', but to the simple fact that, in the tiny early Christian community in Ephesus, Gentile and Jewish Christians were living together in peace. For me, the context makes it clear that Paul is writing about a momentous change in the eternal order of things, not a local event.

Comments made in this context should not have been interpreted at face value, as they often were, within the quite different context, after the fourth century, of a dominant Christian state and a dispersed and powerless Jewish minority.[50]

As Cardinal Ratzinger (later Benedict XVI) wrote, 'the reproofs addressed to Jews in the New Testament are neither more frequent nor more virulent than the accusations against Israel in the Law and the Prophets, at the heart of the Old Testament itself.'[51] God expects a higher standard of those whom he has blessed, whether

---

[50] The beginnings of Christian anti-Judaism in Raymond Brown, Introduction to the New Testament p.166–167
'In the Christian picture of what was done to Jesus, at first there was nothing anti-Jewish in depicting the role of the Jewish authorities in his death; for Jesus and his disciples on one side and the Jewish Sanhedrin authorities on the other were all Jews. The depiction of those Jews opposed to Jesus as plotting evil was not different from the OT depiction of the wicked plotting against the innocent. For instance, in Wisdom 2:17-21 the wicked contend that if the just one be the son of God, God will defend him; and they resolve to revile him and put him to death. The abuse and travail of Jesus took on the hues of the plaintive hymnist of Ps. 22 and the Suffering Servant of Isaiah 52-53. Were all the Jewish authorities opposed to Jesus in fact evil? No. No more than six hundred years earlier all who disagreed with Jeremiah's policies for Judah were wicked. Yet the OT account portrayed them thus, simplifying their motives and dramatizing their actions. Indeed, some of the most sensitive words in the passion of Jesus are found in Jer. 26 (Note 28, Jeremiah warned that [the priests and the people] were bringing innocent blood on Jerusalem and its citizens). Nevertheless, the account of Jesus's passion was eventually 'heard' in an anti-Jewish way. A major factor was the conversion of Gentiles to the following of Jesus. Sometimes the early Christian communities encountered the hostility of local synagogue leaders, and they saw a parallel between this hostility and the treatment of Jesus by the authorities of his time. Now, however, the issue was no longer on an intraJewish level. That other group, the Jews, were doing these things to us Gentile Christians and were responsible for the death of Jesus.'
[51] Ratzinger. Introduction to 'The Jewish people and their Sacred Scriptures' (22).

they be Christians or Jews. As it is written, 'Of those to whom much has been given, much is demanded' (Lk 12:48).[52] In rabbinical tradition, the sages, the early rabbis, did not reprove the people for, as Jonathan Sacks wrote, 'at times of comfort, the role of the prophet is to warn, at times of trouble [after the destruction of the second Temple and the dispersion of the Jews] the role of the prophet is to bring hope.'[53]

The New Testament

It would seem that, as Edward Kessler wrote, 'The problem of polemic is magnified when New Testament passages are read as if they were 'Christian' arguments against the Jews. To read them in this way is to misread them and to ignore the context of the ministry of the earthly Jesus: first-century Palestinian Judaism.' (2)

'The Gospel of John has been called both the most Jewish and the most anti-Jewish'.[54] Those books of the New Testament that are most involved in Jewish matters, the gospels of Matthew and John and the letter to the Hebrews, tend to be those which contain the harshest anti-Jewish material. The closer the writer feels to other Jews, the more keenly he feels their rejection and the more likely he is to slip into an angry polemical mode addressed to fellow Jews. The writer of the Gospel of John feels bitterly that his

---

[52] Pontifical Biblical Commission (22, article 87).

[53] Jonathan Sacks. *Covenant and conversation, Deuteronomy*. Maggid books, 2019, p. 35 (adapted).

[54] Adele Reinhartz. Introduction to the Gospel of John. In The Jewish Annotated New Testament

community is being excluded from the synagogue (John 9:22, 12:42, 16:2). Moreover the Gospel of John is based on binary contrasts; light and darkness, spirit and flesh, life and death. The Gospel uses two generic words for the Jewish people; Israel or Israelite when the evangelist has something positive to say about them (John 1:47,1:49, 12:13), and 'hoi Ioudiaoi', the Judeans (the Jews), which is used more than seventy times, when the evangelist has something negative to say. As a result he writes some verses which, taken out of context, are among the most hurtful in the New Testament. For example in John 8:44 we find addressed to 'a group of Jews (hoi Ioudiaoi) who believed in him', the stark and offensive words, 'You belong to your father, the devil' (John 8:44). In this particular instance the group criticized is not Jews in general, but a group of his own Jewish followers.[55]

---

[55] The writer of John's gospel deals in binary contrasts. He needed to choose one word the describe the 'good' Jews who believed in Jesus and another for the 'bad' Jews who rejected him. In the Talmud, much later than the Gospel but based on older material, the self-description of the community is as 'Israelites'. The word 'Ioudiaoi' only appears a few times in the Talmud and only in the mouth of Gentiles. In the Dead Sea scrolls, a little earlier than the Gospel, the word 'Ioudiaoi' does not appear at all. Reflecting an earlier usage, presumably anachronistic by the time of the Gospel, 'Ioudiaoi' was used in the Septuagint translation of the Hebrew Bible as a translation to 'yehudim'. To make a comparison, another group who live a diaspora existence are known by outsiders (an exonym) as gypsies, but this name is considered derogatory by members of the group, who call themselves Roma. The words Gypsy and, in John's Gospel the word, 'Ioudiaoi' are derogatory exonyms while the words 'Roma' and 'Israelite' are what the corresponding people choose to call themselves (an endonym).
Shaye J. D. Cohen. Judaism and Jewishness. In, The Jewish annotated New Testament, edited Amy-Jill Levine and Marc Zvi Brettler. Oxford University Press, 2017.

For an informed and authoritative opinion on John's Gospel, one can turn to what the Pontifical Biblical commission comments in 2001 about this Gospel and its treatment of the Jews;

'It has been noted with good reason that much of the Fourth Gospel anticipates the trial of Jesus and gives him the opportunity to defend himself and accuse his accusers. These are often called "the Jews" without further precision, with the result that an unfavourable judgement is associated with that name. But there is no question here of anti-Jewish sentiment, since ... [John's] Gospel recognises that "salvation comes from the Jews" (John 4:22). This manner of speaking only reflects the clear separation that existed between the Christian and Jewish communities [at the time when John's Gospel was written].'[56]

In Matthew's Gospel, especially the Sermon on the Mount, the context seems to be that of a community of Jewish Christians who are slowly being excluded from the synagogue and the communal life of their own Jewish people.[57] That such an exclusion occurred

---

The earliest commentary on John that we have, that of Origen, understands this phrase, 'children of the devil' as referring to any human beings opposed to Christ, not specifically to Jews.
https://www.jcrelations.net/articles/article/children-of-the-devil-john-844-and-its-early-reception.html
Adele Reinhartz. *Children of the Devil*: John 8:44 and its Early Reception. Jewish-Christian Relations 01.12.2022
[56] Pontifical Biblical commission (22) article 76.
[57] The verse in Matthew, 'His blood is on us and on our children! (Matthew 27:25) is a quote from Jeremiah 26:15. It has no implications for other Jews then living, let alone subsequent generations of Jews. Nevertheless, this verse has a subsequent history of interpretation to which we should alert, as Edward

is recorded also from the Jewish side. The most commonly quoted event is the addition to the eighteen benedictions, the Jewish daily prayer, of a new benediction, the Birkat ha-minim.[58] This prayer against heretics is often taken to have been directed against Jewish followers of Christ, though they are not specifically mentioned. This sense of being excluded from their own people seems to be the context for the virulent denunciations of the Pharisees in Matthew 23.

Of more consequence for later Christian anti-Judaism were the writings of Paul. In interpreting Paul's letters we must always consider the communities to which his letters were addressed for, as Paul himself wrote (1 Cor. 9:20-21)[59], he adjusted his message

---

Kessler points out.

[58] The exact history and status of the Birkat ha-minim (the twelfth Benediction) is mired in controversy. The Pontifical Biblical commission wrote (22, article 69), 'The Birkat ha-minim, a synagogal "blessing" (actually, a curse) against non-conformists is often cited. Its dating to 85 is uncertain, and the idea that it was a universal Jewish decree against Christians is almost certainly wrong. But one cannot seriously doubt that at certain times in different places, local synagogues no longer tolerated the presence of Christians, and subjected them to harassment that could even go as far as putting them to death (Jn16:2). Gradually, probably from the beginning of the second century, a formula of "blessing" denouncing heretics or deviants of different sorts was composed to include Christians, and much later, they were the ones specifically targeted. Everywhere, by the end of the second century, the lines of demarcation and division were sharply drawn between Christians and Jews who did not believe in Jesus.'
See also; Ruth Langer. Birkat ha-Minim: *A Jewish curse of Christians?* In, The Jewish annotated New Testament, edited Amy-Jill Levine and Marc Zvi Brettler. Oxford University Press, 2017.
[59] 'To the Jews I became like a Jew, to win the Jews. To those under the law I became like one under the law (though I myself am not under the law), so as to win those under the law.'

according to his hearers.[60] Paul wrote a letter to the gentile
Christian community which he had founded in Galatia (estimated
date of writing 54–55 CE). He wanted to protect his new gentile
Christian converts from those who were insisting that they should
all be circumcised and follow the whole Jewish law with its 613
commandments.[61] This letter was not addressed to Jews but to
gentiles. Paul argues passionately that the Galatians will be saved
by faith, not by following the Jewish law and by circumcision in
particular. In Galatians, chapter four, he enters into a long
argument about the children of Sarah and Hagar. As the Hebrew
Bible sees it, the child of Sarah, Isaac, inherits the covenant given
to Abraham, while the child of Sarah's slave Hagar, Ishmael, does
not. Jews, to this day, take great pride in being children of the
covenant given to Abraham, passed to them through Isaac and his
son Jacob. Paul, however, suggests that, allegorically (Galatians
4:23), Christians are the heirs of Isaac because their belief is based
on faith, while the Jews are the heirs of Ishmael, because their

---

[60] Because its trenchant criticisms are directed against Christian Judaizers and
not Jews, I consider Paul's first letter to the Thessalonians as outside the scope
of this essay. As Karl Rahner put it, 'in his polemics Paul is often simply un-
Christian'. Karl Rahner and Pinchas Lapide. *Encountering Jesus – Encountering
Judaism*. Crossroad. New York, 1987. P.53.

[61] Taking Paul's writings as a whole, he is often interpreted as advising
Christians to follow the ethics of the OT, especially the ten commandments, but
not the ritual laws. However, this distinction is not explicitly found in Paul, or in
any Jewish writer of this period. Have we read it back into Paul, or were Paul's
writings at the origin of this distinction, even if he did not explicitly make it
himself?

Naphtali Meshel. The ancient Israelite sacrificial system: an overview. In, Amy-
Jill Levine, Marc Zvi Brettler, Editors. The Jewish Annotated New Testament.
OUP. USA, 2017.

descent is through the flesh. While Paul carefully says this is an allegory, the suggestion that the Jews are not the heirs of the Abrahamic covenant would have been then, and is now, deeply hurtful to Jews because they pride themselves on God's covenant promise. As Jonathan Sacks writes, 'it feels like being disinherited, violated, robbed of an identity'. But, adds Jonathan Sacks, remember, however, that this letter of Paul's was not addressed to a Jewish but a gentile audience. (1)

Paul returns to the question of the covenant with Israel in his letter to the Romans (probably circa 57 CE). Here he is addressing a community that included both Jewish and gentile Christians. As might be expected, then, this letter includes passages addressed to both groups.

To start with the positive, Paul writes (Romans 9:4) that to the Jews belong 'the adoption, and the glory, and the covenants, and the giving of the Law, and the service of God, and the promises'. Paul puts this expression in the present tense, 'to the Jews belong the covenants'. 'Nostra Aetate', the declaration of the Second Vatican Council which covers relations with the Jews (11), quotes this verse. The sense implied by the wording of Nostra Aetate is that by using the present tense, Paul recognises that the covenant has not been abolished. As 'Nostra Aetate' acknowledges, Paul also wrote that, 'there is no change of mind on God's part about the gifts he has made, or of his choice' (Romans 11:28-29).[62]

---

[62] At Romans 11:2, Paul starts Chapter 11, 'God never abandoned his own

Finally 'Nostra Aetate' remembers Paul's words about the church which draws sustenance from the root of that well-cultivated olive tree [the Jewish people] onto which have been grafted the wild shoots, the Gentiles (Rom. 11:17-24).[63] Paul cautions the gentile Christians in Rome: 'do not consider yourselves [the gentiles] to be superior to those other branches [the Jews]' (Romans 11:18). This warning has been sadly much ignored in the subsequent history of the Christian church.

On the other hand in Romans 9:6-9 Paul returns to his theme in Galatians. It is Christians who are the true heirs of Abraham, writes Paul, because they are the heirs through faith, whereas the Jews are heirs through natural descent, just as Isaac was heir through the promise given to Abraham, and Hagar's son was born by natural descent. Paul hammers home his point quoting Malachi 1:3, 'Jacob I loved, but Esau I hated.'[64]

---

people to whom, ages ago, he had given recognition', before reaching his conclusion in 11:28, 'there is no change of mind on God's part about the gifts he has made, or of his choice'. The theme of Romans 11 is that Israel's hardening of heart is temporary; there will be an eventual restoration.

[63] Nostra Aetate (11) also specifically denies the charge of deicide; that the Jewish people then or now, were responsible for the death of Christ. It states that the Jewish people should not be presented as accursed or rejected by God. It is of note that there is no mention of the Holocaust or Israel in 'Nostra Aetate'.

In 1959 the expression 'faithless Jews' had been removed from the Easter liturgy by John XXIII.

[64] 'I hated Esau' can better be read as a Hebraism, simply emphasising God's preference for Jacob. An example of a similar Hebraism is the verse where Jacob is said to love both Leah and Rachel, then, in the next verse to hate Leah (Genesis 29: 30-31).

In Romans 9-11 Paul debates the place of Israel. Several times the Jews in the audience must have felt encouraged by what Paul was saying, only to find the argument turned against them. Then the gentiles may have felt vindicated, only to be told not to boast (Romans 11:18). One can imagine shouts of joy coming, first from one group in the audience, then from the other. But Paul's concludes the chapters with an expression of awe at the even-handed mercy and unsearchability of God, 'For God has bound everyone over to disobedience so that he may have mercy on them all [both Jews and gentiles]. Oh, the depth of the riches of the wisdom and knowledge of God! How unsearchable his judgments, and his paths beyond tracing out!' (Romans 11:33).

In a later letter of the Pauline cannon, Ephesians (possibly written in the 90s CE), an altogether more relaxed note is struck. Here the communities addressed were probably mostly gentile with the remaining Christian Jews well integrated. In Ephesians it is written that '[Jesus] united Jews and Gentiles into one people when, in his own body on the cross, he broke down the wall of hostility that separated us' (Ephesians 2:14). It is a sad fact of history, as stated in the introduction to this piece, that both Christians and Jews have, at least until recent times, remained safely on their side of the wall, a wall which Christ had already destroyed at such cost to himself.

The Church Fathers

Alas, it was the more negative side of Paul's writings on Israel that were picked up in the writings of the Church Fathers.[65] Cyprian (bishop of Carthage 210–258 CE) developed a contrast between Jacob's two wives, Leah who was weak eyed, and Rachel who was comely. Cyprian saw Leah as the type of the synagogue, Rachel the type of the Church. This, combined with Paul's image of a veil over the eyes of Israel (2 Corinthians 3:14), lead to a medieval iconography of two wives, the beautiful Cristian Church and the synagogue with a blind over her eyes.[66]

Melito of Sardis (140–185 CE), Tertullian (active in Carthage 155–220 CE), John Chrysostom (archbishop of Constantinople 347–407 CE)[67] and Aphrahat (a Syriac Christian from Mosul 280–345 CE) made the final devastating move: the Jews are Cain who, having murdered their brother (this is the charge of deicide), are now condemned to permanent exile (1). This analogy was taken up by Augustine (bishop of Carthage 354 – 430 CE). For Augustine, the Jews, like Cain, were both cursed by God to wander, yet protected by him. They were 'witnesses' preserved by God to demonstrate the truth of the Old Testament.[68] The analogy with Cain was

---

[65] This history is presented in greater detail at;
https://en.wikipedia.org/wiki/Anti-Judaism
[66] As on the facade of the RC cathedral in Strasbourg and Notre-Dame in Paris.
[67] One of Chrysostom's controversial passages occurs in a sermon where he is trying to persuade his Christian congregation not to attend church services. Edward Kessler (2) p.5.
[68] Edward Kessler (2) p.51.

quoted much later in the mediaeval decrees of expulsion of the Jews from various places, starting in England in 1290. So far, we have been talking of Christian anti-Judaism. But shortly after the expulsion of the Jews from Spain (1492) we see the beginning of anti-Semitism. Jews who had converted and remained in Spain began to experience discrimination and even persecution, not because of their religion, but because they, or their ancestors, had been Jews. Thus began the Spanish obsession with 'limpieza di sangre'.

We should not forget, however, that Christian anti-Judaism itself led to real and repeated violence, to the massacres during the First Crusade, to the expulsions and to many other violent incidents.

The Holocaust or Shoah

The Holocaust, or Shoah to the Jews, was the Nazi regime's meticulously planned and almost successful extermination by murder of the European Jews. As well as six million Jews, millions of Poles, Russians, Gypsies, homosexuals and other groups considered 'subhuman' were also murdered. In August 1942, seven hundred or so Jews from my mother's village of Bobowa, Gorlice County, Poland[69] were shot in the Garbacz forest just south of the

---

[69] https://en.wikipedia.org/wiki/Bobowa

village.[70] After the war a modest memorial was erected at the site. There were only a handful of survivors. (6)

A

Ceramic model of the memorial to the Jews of the Bobowa ghetto. After the war the memorial was erected in Garbacz forest. (4)

The inscription, translated into English, reads: 'In this mass grave / rest nearly 1000 jews / from Gorlice and Bobowa: / victims of hitlerian beastly slaughter / on august 14, 1942. / The erection of this monument / on this holy ground / was done by Nachum Ormanier / and Jakub Peller, the chairman of the/ county Jewish committee of Gorlice.'

---

[70] It was part of that 'holocaust by bullets', the killing of circa 1.5 million Jews that preceded the better-known industrialised killing of the death camps (5), (25).

The Second Vatican Council and subsequent developments[71]

Pope John XXIII (1881–1963) called the second Vatican council in 1962. He had been familiar with the plight of the Jews in war time Istanbul.[72] In 1960, he had met Jules Isaac (1877 – 1963 CE) [73] a prominent French Jewish historian who had lost most of his family during the Holocaust and had put together a history of anti-Jewish teachings in the Western church (3). The spirit of John XXIII is behind the Vatican document on relations with the Jews, 'Nostra Aetate' (11), although it was published after his death, when Paul VI was Pope. This document, for the first time, clearly stated that, in the eyes of the Catholic church, God was faithful to his promises and in particular to his covenant with the Jews. As discussed above this statement was explicitly based on Romans 9 where Paul refers to God's covenant with the Jews in the present tense.[74]

---

[71] In this section I focus on the Roman Catholic church. A similar story can be told about the Protestant churches, and is to be found in Edward Keller (2).

[72] Angelo Roncalli, later John XXIII, is recorded as 'providing thousands of fake baptismal certificates', and helping 'tens of thousands' of Jews escape to Palestine from Istanbul during the war, going against church policy, which discouraged Jewish emigration to Palestine. Edward Kessler (2) p.135. https://www.jewishvirtuallibrary.org/preliminary-report-on-the-vatican-during-the-holocaust-october-2000-2

[73] https://en.wikipedia.org/wiki/Jules_Isaac

[74] This is sometimes called, 'Dual covenant theology' as opposed to supersessionism (annulling some of the Old Covenant laws) or to full abrogation of the covenants (annulling all Old Covenant laws). Full abrogation of the covenant is sometimes supported by reference to Hebrews 8:13. In fact this verse only states that the old covenant will disappear (be abrogated)

Pontiffs since have stuck to this line, in particular John Paul II who had lived through the period when the Holocaust was happening in Poland and one of whose Jewish school friends survived. In 1994, in a move of great significance to Jewish people, the Vatican recognised the state of Israel. In 1997 John Paul II wrote, 'This people [the Jewish people] perseveres in spite of everything because they are the people of the Covenant, and despite human infidelities, the Lord is faithful to his Covenant' (18). Where Paul had written in Romans that 'not all descendants of Abraham count as his children' (Romans 9:6-7), John Paul II countered in 'We

---

'soon'. Hebrews 7:15-19, on the other hand, does suggest that the Law has been replaced. https://en.wikipedia.org/wiki/Dual-covenant_theology#cite_note-14

Hebrews is commonly thought to be addressed to a community of Jewish priests. The writer is urging them not to return to the priestly sacrificial system, the only thing they had known before they met Christ. The letter abounds in detailed and obscure – to us -refences to the sacrificial rites in the Torah. The tone of the whole letter is rather like the president of a society of steam train enthusiasts urging them, with multiple technical references, that diesel is better in every detailed respect and that they must not return to the steam engines for which they are nostalgic. For the writer of Hebrews Jesus is the antitype, the fulfilment, of all the many different sorts of sacrifice in the Torah. These sacrifices are all explained as types, foreshadowings of the sacrifice of Christ. It is not surprising that such a letter contains the only explicit supersessionist theology in the NT.

Naphtali Meshel. The ancient Israelite sacrificial system: an overview. In, Amy-Jill Levine, Marc Zvi Brettler, Editors. The Jewish Annotated New Testament. OUP. USA, 2017.

There is a discussion by Cardinal Walter Casper at;
https://www.bc.edu/content/dam/files/research_sites/cjl/texts/cjrelations/resources/articles/kasper_dominus_iesus.htm Supersessionism, though that name was not used, was the position of the Catholic church until Vatican II. According to Edward Kessler, the RC church now has a 'single covenant' theology. For a detailed discussion of developments since Vatican II see;
https://en.wikipedia.org/wiki/Supersessionism#cite_note-vatican.va-37

Remember – A Reflection on the Shoah' (1998) that both Jews and Christians, 'adore the one Creator and Lord and have a common father in faith, Abraham.' (19). That document did not mention repentance, but, two years later (2000), John Paul II presided over a millennial liturgy of repentance, including specifically repentance for Christian teaching against the Jews and Judaism and for the failure of the Church during the Shoah.[75] Also in 2000 John Paul II visited Israel. He visited Yad Vashem and wept. His unscripted insertion of a prayer into the Western Wall of the Temple is remembered by Jewish people to this day.[76]

For Jonathan Sacks, particularly moving was Pope Francis I's 2013 statement in the leading Italian daily newspaper 'La Repubblica' (24). 'What I can say to you,' wrote Francis, 'with the Apostle Paul, is that God's fidelity to the close covenant with Israel never failed and that, through the terrible trials of these centuries, the Jews have kept their faith in God. And for this, we shall never be sufficiently grateful to them as Church, but also as humanity.' Here Pope Francis not only repeats the understanding of Vatican II that God is faithful to his covenant with Israel, but adds that the Church is grateful to Israel for her faith in God despite her terrible trials.

---

[75] Edward Kessler (2) p.142

[76] The prayer reads; 'God of our fathers, / you chose Abraham and his descendants / to bring your Name to the Nations: / we are deeply saddened by the behaviour of those / who in the course of history / have caused these children of yours to suffer, / and asking your forgiveness we wish to commit ourselves / to genuine brotherhood / with the people of the Covenant. 26 March 2000.

Pope Francis is here venturing forth from his safe Catholic territory across the dividing wall destroyed in Christ, and taking a step towards the Jewish people, a step which Rabbi Jonathan Sacks warmly appreciates in his book (1).[77]

The Anglican response to the Holocaust

The Anglican communion bears no direct responsibility for the Holocaust, nor did the Holocaust occur on territories controlled by the British government. Nevertheless the Anglican communion has responded in its own particular way to these tragic events, as have the other Protestant denominations. Before World War II, James Parkes (1896–1981), an Anglican clergyman, devoted his life to mobilising British opinion on behalf of Jewish victims of the anti-Semitic persecution in Europe.[78] He had personally witnessed this persecution while working in Europe before the war. His magnum opus was 'The Conflict of the Church and the Synagogue: A Study in the Origins of Antisemitism. A history of antisemitism'

---

[77] In 'Christian theology: an introduction' Alistair McGrath makes a distinction between revelatory and salvationist views of inclusivity. Inclusivity is that belief by some Christians that the Christian God may be found in other religions. A revelatory view is the view that something of God may be revealed in non-Christian religions. All Christians necessarily believe this of Judaism, from which Christianity developed. 'Nostra Aetate' and the theology of the Second Vatican council went no further than this. Here Pope Francis at least hints that Israel's faith in God may be salvific for Jewish people. The Jesuit theologian, Karl Rahner, had maintained in his 'theological investigations' with his theory of 'unknown Christians' that non-Christian religions had a salvific element. This was not incorporated into Vatican II, but nor, so far as I know, has it been condemned.

[78] https://en.wikipedia.org/wiki/James_Parkes_(priest)

(1934).[79] He was instrumental in forming the 'Council of Christians and Jews' (CCJ) of which Archbishop Temple and the chief Rabbi Joseph Hertz were first co-presidents.[80],[81] Archbishop Temple spoke out boldly against the Holocaust while WWII was still on-going. All subsequent archbishops have continued in this role, as co-presidents with the Chief Rabbi. In a sad episode, Roman Catholics left the CCJ between 1954 and 1962 due to Vatican concern about 'indifferentism'.[82] A formal response from the Anglican communion came in a report to the 1988 Lambeth Conference, 'Jews, Christians and Muslims, the way of dialogue'.[83] The heart of the report reads:

'Through catechism, teaching of school children, and Christian preaching, the Jewish people have been misrepresented and caricatured. Even the Gospels have, at times, been used to malign and denigrate the Jewish people. Anti-Jewish prejudice promulgated by leaders of Church and State has led to persecution,

---

[79] James Parker. The Conflict of the Church and the Synagogue: A Study in the Origins of Antisemitism. A history of antisemitism.' London: Soncino Press, 1934

[80] For Rabbi Hertz see; https://en.wikipedia.org/wiki/Joseph_Hertz
[81] The website is https://ccj.org.uk
For a useful history of the CCJ and the involvement in its formation of other Christian denominations, see;
https://en.wikipedia.org/wiki/Council_of_Christians_and_Jews
The 'International council of Christians and Jews' has on-line magazine 'Jewish Christian relations' at;
https://www.iccj.org/article/jcrelationsnet-may-edition-online-8-1.html
[82] https://en.wikipedia.org/wiki/Indifferentism
[83] An extract can be found at;
https://www.jcrelations.net/statements/statement/jews-christians-and-muslims-the-way-of-dialogue.html

pogrom and finally, provided the soil in which the evil weed of Nazism was able to take root and spread its poison. The Nazis were driven by a pagan philosophy, which had as its ultimate aim the destruction of Christianity itself. But how did it take hold? The systematic extermination of six million Jews and the wiping out of a whole culture must bring about in Christianity a profound and painful re-examination of its relationship with Judaism. In order to combat centuries of anti-Jewish teaching and practice, Christians must develop programmes of teaching, preaching, and common social action which eradicate prejudice and promote dialogue.'[84]

On the vexed question of conversion of the Jews as opposed to dialogue, the report contains these careful words, 'All these approaches, however, share a common concern to be sensitive about Judaism, to reject all proselytising, that is, aggressive and manipulative attempts to convert, and, of course, any hint of antisemitism. Further, Jews, Muslims and Christians share a common mission.' This report, it may be noted, preceded by some years, Pope John Paul II's millennial liturgy of repentance in 2000. A particular high point of Jewish-Anglican relations was Rabbi Jonathan Sacks addressing, on the subject of covenant, the many

---

[84] The 2008 Synod went further. In relation to the Jews and their scriptures it said: 'The divine word generates for us Christians an equally intense encounter with the Jewish people, who are intimately bound through the common recognition and love for the Scripture of the Old Testament... Every page of the Jewish Scriptures enlightens the mystery of God and of man... These are a way of dialogue with the chosen people ... and they allow us to enrich our interpretation of the Sacred Scriptures with the fruitful resources of the Hebrew exegetical tradition.

bishops attending the 2008 Lambeth meeting of the Anglican communion.[85],[86]

A Jewish perspective

But I would maintain that Sacks, both in his book 'Not in God's name' and in his other works, has taken a step towards Christians. This he has done by emphasising, and bringing to a non-Jewish audience, a special understanding of the covenants of God. This understanding can already be found in the Babylonian Talmud (written circa 200–500 CE).[87] In the Hebrew Bible the covenant with Noah is mentioned rather briefly and has been largely ignored by Christian theology. But in the Talmud this passage is much expanded. For Sacks the covenant with Noah is a covenant with all peoples, both the gentile nations and the Jewish people, in fact the whole creation.[88] This first covenant applies the Noahide laws of justice to all, and therefore this is the only covenant which applies to the Gentiles. The later covenant with Abraham is for the Jews

---

[85] These few words on Anglicanism and the Holocaust draw largely on Edward Kessel's book, *An introduction to Jewish-Christian relations*.

[86] This address can be watched, and I would strongly recommend you to do so; https://www.rabbisacks.org/videos/faith-and-fate-the-lambeth-conference-address/

[87] Babylonian Talmud Sanhedrin 56a-b and Tosefta Avodah Zarah 8:4.

[88] In Genesis the Noahide covenant is a covenant with the whole creation, not just human beings. This theme of a covenant with the whole cosmos is applied to the New Covenant in Ephesians.

alone. God has chosen a special way for Israel. But when God chooses, writes Jonathan Sacks, he does not reject. He has a special way for each nation. Jonathan Sacks explicitly applies the Noahide covenant to Christians, something many earlier Jewish commentators had been reluctant to do. [89] Incidentally, this understanding of the Noahide covenant being the one which applies to the gentiles seems to lie behind the decision of the Council of Jerusalem (Acts 15: 19-21). Here James appears to decide that Gentile converts need only follow the Noahide laws (or something rather like them) and do not need to follow the full Mosaic law.

Conclusion

Thus, as I see it, Popes John XXIII, John Paul II and Francis I on the one hand, and Jules Isaac, Edward Kessler and Rabbi Jonathan Sacks on the other, as well as many others, have taken the first steps across that dividing wall between Jews and Gentiles which was destroyed so long ago. Taking this step they have found,

---

[89] As Russian Wikipedia notes; 'The inclusion of Christians among the Noahides caused controversy in the Jewish community until the end of the Middle Ages, since from the point of view of Judaism, the worship of Jesus of Nazareth and the dogma of the Trinity of God is a violation of the principle of monotheism and is idolatry [Avodah Zarah]. Currently, the prevailing opinion is that Christians are Noahides, since the doctrine of the Trinity falls into the category of 'shituf' (joining God with auxiliary "images" without direct idolatry) and is not forbidden for non-Jews.'
https://ru.wikipedia.org/wiki/%D0%A1%D0%B5%D0%BC%D1%8C_%D0%B7%D0%B0%D0%BA%D0%BE%D0%BD%D0%BE%D0%B2_%D0%BF%D0%BE%D1%82%D0%BE%D0%BC%D0%BA%D0%BE%D0%B2_%D0%9D%D0%BE%D1%8F
Maimonides (1138-1204), who lived in Islamic lands all his life, applied the Noahide covenant to Islam but not Christianity. Edward Kessler (2).

perhaps to their surprise, that, on the other side, there are people capable of being kind and thoughtful, people rather like themselves, people made, just as they are, in the image of God.

Questions

1) Have you ever witnessed / experienced Christian anti-Judaism or anti-Semitism?
2) Have you ever responded to it, and, if so, how?
3) How do you think you would respond now?
4) Can the Jewish-Christian dialogue teach us anything about ecumenical dialogue, or dialogue with other religions?

Bibliography

1)   Rabbi Jonathan Sacks. *Not in God's Name: Confronting Religious Violence*. London. Hodder and Stoughton, 2016.

2) Edward Kessler. *An Introduction to Jewish-Christian Relations*. Cambridge University Press, 2010.

3) Jules Isaac. *Jésus et les Juifs*. Paris. Albin Michel, 1948.

On the 'Holocaust by bullets' and the massacre of the Jews of Bobowa;

4)   Samuel P. Oliner. *Restless memories, recollections of the Holocaust years*. Judah L. Magnes Museum, Berkeley, California, 1979

5) Father Patrick Desbois. The Holocaust by Bullets: A Priest's Journey to Uncover the   Truth Behind the Murder of 1.5 Million Jews. St. Martin's Griffin,, 2009.

6)   Gervase Vernon. Belonging and betrayal. Independently published, 2003.

7)   Sir Martin Gilbert. *The Boys: Triumph Over Adversity*. London. Phoenix 2003

Internet Resources *(the words in italics are quotes from the documents concerned);*

This section includes links, in date order, to the more important documents issued by the Roman Catholic church on Jewish-

Christian relations since the second Vatican council, as well as other relevant documents.

8) An excellent overview of post WWII Catholic- Jewish relations is, 'Milestones in Modern Jewish-Christian Relations' Dec 29, 2018. Compiled by Sr. Lucy Thorson, NDS and Murray Watson

   https://www.notredamedesion.org/?s=milestones

   There is a very good and detailed talk on the subject of Vatican II and the Jews based on this material by Sr Margaret Shepherd, secretary to the Committee for Catholic – Jewish Relations, a Sister of Sion at:

   https://www.whatgoodnews.org/vatican-ii-talks

9) 1947. The ten points of Seelisburg. Post war meeting of the 'International Conference of Christians and Jews' (ICCJ).

   https://en.wikipedia.org/wiki/Seelisberg_Conference

10) 1948. WCC. Report on the Christian approach to the Jews.

   https://www.oikoumene.org/resources/documents/concerns-of-the-churches-the-christian-approach-to-the-jews

11) 1965. 'Nostra Aetate'. Declaration on the relation of the church to non-Christian religions 'Nostra aetate' proclaimed by his holiness Pope Paul VI.

    The English text is at;

    http://www.vatican.va/archive/hist_councils/ii_vatican_council/documents/vat-ii_decl_19651028_nostra-aetate_en.html

12) 1975. Guidelines and Suggestions for Implementing the Conciliar Declaration Nostra Aetate https://www.ccjr.us/dialogika-resources/documents-and-statements/roman-catholic/vatican-curia/guidelines

13) 1980. Meeting of John Paul II with the Representatives of the Jewish Community, Mainz, Section 3, 17 November 1980. Here John Paul II spoke of *'a covenant never revoked'.* https://www.vatican.va/content/john-paul-ii/it/speeches/1980/november/documents/hf_jp_ii_spe_198 01117_ebrei-magonza.html

14) 1985. Notes on the Correct Way to Present the Jews and Judaism in Preaching and Catechesis in the Roman Catholic Church. *'The permanence of Israel (while so many ancient people have disappeared without trace) is a historic fact and a sign to be interpreted within God's design.'* https://www.bc.edu/content/dam/files/research_sites/cjl/text s/cjrelations/resources/documents/catholic/Vatican_Notes.h tm

15) 1986. Documentation Catholique 83 (1986) 437. John Paul II, addressing the Jewish communities of Italy during a visit to the synagogue of Rome, declared: *"You are our favoured brothers and, in a certain sense, one can say our elder brothers".*

https://www.nytimes.com/1986/04/14/world/text-of-pope-s-speech-at-rome-synagogue-you-are-our-elder-brothers.html

16) 1988. Jews, Christians and Muslims: The Way of Dialogue. A document from the Anglican communion. https://nifcon.anglicancommunion.org/media/129614/lam88_ap6.pdf

17) 1992. Catechism of the Catholic Church. Para 63, *'Israel is the priestly people of God, 'called by the name of the Lord' and 'the first to hear the word of God' (Dt. 28:10), the people of 'elder brethren' in the faith of Abraham.'* Para 839, *'the Jewish faith, unlike other non-Christian religions, is already a response to God's revelation'.*

18) 1997. Address of His Holiness Pope John Paul II to a symposium on the roots of anti-Judaism http://www.vatican.va/content/john-paul-ii/en/speeches/1997/october/documents/hf_jp-ii_spe_19971031_com-teologica.html

19) 1998. The text of 'We Remember – A Reflection on the Shoah' is at; https://www.jewishvirtuallibrary.org/quot-we-remember-quot-vatican-reflection-on-the-shoah Other documents concerning the Vatican and the Holocaust can be found in the Jewish Virtual Library; https://www.jewishvirtuallibrary.org/the-vatican-and-the-holocaust

20) 2000. Dabru Emet. A Jewish Statement on Christians and Christianity which appeared as a full-page advert in the New York Times.

https://icjs.org/dabru-emet-text/

21) 2001. Church and Israel: A Contribution from the Reformation Churches in Europe to the Relationship between Christians and Jews

https://www.jcrelations.net/fr/article/church-and-israel-a-contribution-from-the-reformation-churches-in-europe-to-the-relationship-between-christians-and-jews.pdf

22) 2001. The Jewish people and their Sacred Scriptures in the Christian Bible. The Pontifical Biblical Commission. *The Jewish messianic expectation is not in vain'.*

https://www.vatican.va/roman_curia/congregations/cfaith/pcb_documents/rc_con_cfaith_doc_20020212_popolo-ebraico_en.html

23) 2004. Congregation for Roman Catholic Bishops, Directory for the pastoral ministry of bishops 2004. *'[The bishop] should be vigilant that sacred ministers receive an adequate formation regarding the Jewish religion and its relation to Christianity.'*

http://www.vatican.va/roman_curia/congregations/cbishops/documents/rc_con_cbishops_doc_20040222_apostolorum-successores_en.html

24) 2009 International Council of Christians and Jews issues "A Time For Recommitment" (The Twelve Points of Berlin)

https://www.iccj.org/fileadmin/ICCJ/pdf-Dateien/12points_Berlin_engl.pdf

The above document refers back to the 1947 'The ten points of Seelisburg' (see above).

25) 2013. The full English text of the article by Pope Francis in La Repubblica is at;

https://www.repubblica.it/cultura/2013/09/11/news/the_pope_s_letter-66336961/

26) 2015. Pontifical Council for Christian Unity. "The gifts and the calling of god are irrevocable" (Rom 11:29) A Reflection on Theological Questions Pertaining to Catholic-Jewish Relations on the Occasion of the 50th Anniversary of "Nostra Aetate" (No. 4)

http://www.christianunity.va/content/unitacristiani/en/commissione-per-i-rapporti-religiosi-con-l-ebraismo/commissione-per-i-rapporti-religiosi-con-l-ebraismo-crre/documenti-della-commissione/en.html

'Jews who believe in one God,' should be approached 'in a different manner from that to people of other religions... In concrete terms this means that the Catholic church neither conducts nor supports any specific institutional mission work directed towards the Jews.'

A summary can be found at:

https://sioncentre.org/the-gift-and-calling-of-god-are-irrevocable/

27) For the 'Holocaust by bullets' see:

https://en.wikipedia.org/wiki/Holocaust_by_Bullets

Yahad In-Unum is an organisation devoted to studying the 'Holocaust by bullets'. There is a map of Poland at

https://www.yahadinunum.org/

.

6. WEEK 5. ROMANS 9-11. IS GOD FAITHFUL TO HIS PROMISES?

Principles of the course so far

1) First get to know somebody (or some group) and learn to love them for themselves, before you judge them. This applies to all groups, not just Jews.

2) You should check that your theology is consistent with scripture. **But another way of checking your theology is by its effects.**[90] If your theology leads to hatred and violence or feelings of guilt and exclusion (often experienced by a marginalised group, and you will need to ask them), then your theology is somehow wrong. If it leads to joy, love and justice, your theology is more likely right. (Jim Packer also says something a bit like this).

---

[90] This idea comes from; Jesper Svartvik. *Reconciliation and Transformation, Reconsidering Christian theologies of the Cross.* Cascade Books, 2021.

The Holocaust was the industrialised murder between 1941 and 1945 by the antisemitic, non-Christian Nazi government of six million Jews (about one in three of the Jews then alive) and of many other people: Poles, Russians, Gypsies, homosexuals, Jehovah's witnesses and so on. The crucial word in the preceding sentence is 'others'. If we define ourselves against 'others', then we can move from ignorance of the other to hatred, from hatred to murder and from murder to industrialised killing as the Nazis did and others have done since.[91]

What, you might ask, is the connection of the Holocaust with Romans 9-11? There is a twofold connection. One I will mention now, the other at the end. The first connection is this: anti-Semitism is prejudice against Jews **as a race**, whose terrible fruit was the Holocaust. But one of the roots of anti-Semitism is Christian anti-Judaism, the disparagement, the contempt, of Judaism **as a religion**, which we looked at last week. The classic authors of Christian anti- Judaism, such as Augustine, often based their opinions on Paul and in particular Romans 9-11. Yet some verses in Romans 9-11, such as Romans 11:29, 'the gifts and the calling of God [to Israel] are irrevocable' are key texts for reversing this legacy.[92]

---

[91] Black eyed peas. Where is the love? If you only have love for your own race, then you learn to discriminate'.
https://www.youtube.com/watch?v=FotCW5OIFZc
[92] 'The letter of Paul to the Romans'. Mark D. Nanos. Jewish annotated NT. This author sees a Paul within Judaism. Both Jew and gentile will be saved in an imminent return of Christ. Gentiles must turn from idolatry to Israel's God (first

While Paul writes about Judaism in many places in his letters, Romans 9-11 is his longest and most sustained examination of the relationship between the gentile followers of Christ and the Judaism of his day. One reading of this passage is to define Christianity as against Judaism. The Christian church supersedes Israel as the recipient of God's covenant promises, a view known as supersessionism. I wish to offer a different reading which was suggested to me by archbishop Rowan Williams's book on Paul.[93]

In Romans 9-11, Paul asks the question, 'How is justification by faith, through Christ (which Paul sets out in Romans 1-4) reconcilable with God's irrevocable promises to Israel? (Found throughout the OT)' Paul argues first one side of the case (that God's promises to Israel are irrevocable), then the other (that the followers of Jesus have replaced Israel), before finally ending triumphantly with a conclusion that takes things further without

---

five commandments of the decalogue) and also follow the next five commandments (Romans 13:8-9, I Cor. 7:19), summarised in the 'Law of love for the neighbour', but they need not undergo circumcision or follow the Torah, these are given to Jews only. Gentiles are saved as gentiles, not as Jews (Romans 15:10-12). With combative rhetoric Paul writes against other Christians, Judaizers, who would force his converts to be circumcised. In none of his letters, which were written to gentiles, does Paul encourage Jews to cease following the Torah. He is clear, however, that the redemption of the Jews does not come from the Torah, but from Christ.

[93] Rowan Williams. *Meeting God in Paul*. SPCK, 2015.

negating the arguments on either side.[94],[95],[96]. Paul's purpose in this passage, I would suggest, is to bring both sides (Jewish and gentile Christians) to a common mind. I may be wrong. But have some Christian interpreters just heard one side of the argument and used it to define Christianity as a religion in opposition to Judaism?

Paul is deeply emotionally involved in both sides of the argument. But his triumphant conclusion at the end of this passage (Romans 11: 32-36) is not in favour of either one side of the argument or the

---

[94] We do not know if the congregation at Rome contained both gentile and Jewish followers of Christ, or whether Paul had any personal knowledge of the make-up of the congregation. But it really does not matter whether Paul is debating within his own mind, or trying to persuade a mixed congregation. Either way, Paul is first putting one side of the argument, then the other, before coming to a conclusion that goes beyond the initial arguments without invalidating them.

[95]Some maintain that this method of argument is a Graeco-Roman diatribe? We can call the first argument the thesis, the second the antithesis and the conclusion the synthesis Using Hegel's terminology of dialectic, more familiar to us, perhaps, than Graeco-Roman diatribe.

From Wikipedia; 'A noted historical example of a religious diatribe can be found in Paul's Epistle to the Romans. With respect to that usage, a diatribe is described as an oration in which the speaker seeks to persuade an audience by debating an imaginary opponent, "typically using second person singular". The speaker "raises hypothetical questions and responds to them or states false conclusions and goes on to refute them"'. Arland J. Hultgren, Paul's Letter to the Romans: A Commentary (2011), p. 85.

R Bultmann's doctoral dissertation was on the diatribe in Paul. Brown. An introduction to the NT. p. 89 n 4.

[96] Rowan Williams, 'Meeting Paul' loc269, 'You can read the whole of the letter to the Romans and hear it as Paul turning his head from side to side, saying to Jew and Gentile alike, 'You think you have grounds for feeling superior; let me tell you you're not. Just because I'm telling them that they are not superior, don't go thinking you are.'

other, but that all, Jew and gentile alike, depend on the mercy of God.

Romans 9-11 is read at this point

Four readers are needed. The text is in week 5b. One person reads the pieces printed in *italics* (the thesis: that God's promises to Israel have not been revoked), which would rejoice any Jewish followers of Christ in the audience, a second person reads the pieces written in normal type (the anti-thesis: that the gentile followers of Jesus are replacing Israel), at which point you can imagine gentile followers of Christ in the audience cheering. A third person reads the pieces written in **bold** which are Paul's synthesis and his own conclusions, as I see them. Finally, a fourth person reads the titles and subtitles, which editors of the Bible have added to Paul's text.

As you listened, I hope you heard the almost regular pattern, *italics*, normal type, **bold**: thesis, antithesis, synthesis. I hope you understood that part of Paul's purpose was to bring Jewish and gentile followers of Christ together; to knock their heads together and bring them to a common mind. Indeed, in the next chapter of Romans, Paul pleads with his readers, 'Be of the same mind one toward another' (Romans 121:16 KJV). You can also see that, if the reader chooses just to hear the 'normal type' passages, the anti-thesis, he can get a reading of Christianity as defined against Judaism, a Christianity for which Judaism is 'the other'. For me, however, to paraphrase John Paul II, Judaism is not the other, but the brother, indeed the elder brother of Christianity.[97]

Tom Wright, in his excellent commentary, 'Paul for everyone: Romans' gives a straightforward exegesis of this passage. How can we say that God is faithful to his promises to Israel? Firstly, on previous occasions, such as the exile in Babylon, the prophets had explained that God's promise is not addressed to the whole of Israel, but to a faithful remnant. This pattern of promise and curse goes back to the covenantal promises in Genesis. Secondly Paul states that the promise is not addressed to the physical descendants of Israel (just as it was not addressed to all the physical descendants of Abraham), but to the descendants in faith.[98] The

---

[97] 1986. Documentation Catholique 83 (1986) 437. John Paul II, addressing the Jewish communities of Italy during a visit to the synagogue of Rome, declared: "You are our favoured brothers and, in a certain sense, one can say our elder brothers."
https://www.nytimes.com/1986/04/14/world/text-of-pope-s-speech-at-rome-synagogue-you-are-our-elder-brothers.html
This formula, used by John Paul II has an in-built ambiguity. In the parable of the prodigal son, God is calling the elder brother, the pharisees to whom the parable is addressed, to the party, but we are not told the outcome. As Christians see it, God is still calling Israel. They are not being called to abandon the Law, but to recognise Jesus as Messiah.
[98] Of note this is the argument which Maimonides uses in a letter concerning a convert to the Jewish faith. 'Rambam's Letter to Obadiah the Convert'. In it Maimonides argues that, 'whoever adopts Judaism and confesses the unity of the Divine Name' may consider Abraham as his father.
http://www.ashokkarra.com/2010/07/maimonides-letter-to-obadiah-the-proselyte/

gentiles will be gathered at first, making Israel jealous, then a remnant of Israel will be gathered in.[99]

For some (not Tom Wright or Rowan Williams) the Christian church takes over (supersedes) the promises made to Israel; the position known as supersessionism. This was the generally understood position of the RC church until Vatican II (1962-1965). Then the RC church, in horror at the enormity of the Holocaust of which one root was Christian anti-Judaism, abandoned this position in the document 'Nostra Aetate' (1965), which set out the relations of the RC church to non-Christian faiths.[100]

Both Christianity and Rabbinical Judaism have a 2000-year history. Pope Francis wrote in 2013 reflecting on this history and referring specifically to the Holocaust, **'What I can say to you [the Jewish people], with the Apostle Paul, is that God's fidelity to the close covenant with Israel never failed and that, through the terrible trials of these centuries, the Jews have kept their faith in God. And for this, we shall never be sufficiently grateful to them as Church, but also as humanity.'**[101]

---

[99] In the closing verses, I do not interpret Paul's vision of a conversion of Israel 'now' (Romans 11:31) as a precise chronology. Paul foresaw an imminent conversion of a 'remnant' of Israel, starting 'now', to be followed by a Second Coming within his lifetime. This has not happened. God's sense of time is notoriously different from ours. It is unwise to interpret the prophecies in scripture, such as those in Revelation, in a literal sense.

[100] 'Nostra Aetate' was written by three priests of whom two, John M. Oesterreicher and Bruno Hussar, were Jewish converts to Catholicism.

[101] 2013. The full English text of the article by Pope Francis in *La Repubblica* is at; https://www.repubblica.it/cultura/2013/09/11/news/the_pope_s_letter-

Here Pope Francis is arguing for a new relationship with contemporary Judaism, one based on gratitude rather than contempt. He is admiring the faithfulness of the Jews, not writing that Jews can be saved in a separate way from Christians. However, like Paul, he emphasises that God is faithful to his covenant with the Jews. In this statement, he leaves the salvation of the Jews to the justice and mercy of God, as Paul does in the conclusion of Romans 11.

What Paul could not have foreseen was a two-thousand-year history of Christians persecuting Jews once Christians had become dominant politically. If Jews have their ears closed now to the message of Christ because of this two-thousand-year history of persecution by Christians, this should lead us as Christians to a deep repentance.

Now I come to the second connection between Romans 9–11 and the Holocaust. How can we square God's promises to Israel, repeated throughout the OT (and which Paul is trying to reconcile in Romans 9–11 with justification by faith) with the virtual extermination of European Jewry, in conditions of unbelievable cruelty, in WWII?

This is the problem we Europeans wrestle with today, just as Paul wrestled with an apparent failure of God's irrevocable promises to Israel in his own day, in his own context. Elie Wiesel, himself a

66336961/

survivor of the Holocaust, expresses this struggle in the poem, 'Never Shall I Forget';[102]

'Never shall I forget that night, the first night in camp, that turned my life into one

long night seven times sealed.

Never shall I forget that smoke.

Never shall I forget the small faces of the children whose bodies I saw transformed

into smoke under a silent sky.

Never shall I forget those flames that consumed my faith for ever.

Never shall I forget the nocturnal silence that deprived me for all eternity of the

desire to live.

Never shall I forget those moments that murdered my God and my soul and

turned my dreams to ashes.

Never shall I forget those things, even were I condemned to live

---

[102] From his book, *Night*. https://www.hmd.org.uk/wp-content/uploads/2018/06/Never-Shall-I-Forget.pdf

as long as God Himself.

Never.'

(Pause)

This poem does not represent Wiesel's outlook taken as a whole. In his speech accepting the Nobel peace prize he said, 'But I have faith. Faith in the God of Abraham, Isaac, and Jacob, and even in His creation.'[103] Rather this poem is a shout of protest addressed to God. Similar passages can be found in the Psalms. Christ himself on the cross prayed, 'My God, my God, why have you forsaken me?'

Who was silent during the Holocaust? Was God the one who was silent, as Wiesel wrote, or were we, the bystanders, the ones who were silent?[104] Was Christ himself one of the victims as Wiesel hints in a famous passage further in the same book? This hint is developed in the writings of Jürgen Moltmann, a German Reformed Theologian, who writes of a God suffering with humanity.

Is God silent now during the current man-made famine in Afghanistan, during the war in Ukraine, is he silent while our government is scapegoating asylum seekers, or are we the ones

---

[103]https://www.acpsd.net/site/handlers/filedownload.ashx?moduleinstanceid=69275&dataid=142567&FileName=Elie%20Wiesel%20%20Night%20FULL%20TEXT.pdf

[104] Richard Breitman. *Official Secrets: What the Nazis Planned, What the British and Americans Knew.* Farrar, Straus & Giroux, 1998. ISBN 0-8090-3819-6

who are silent when we should be shouting? Is it God who is unfaithful to his promises, or are we the ones who are unfaithful to our promises?

Yes, God is faithful. Christ is risen, and it is the risen Christ who calls us to be his voice of peace and reconciliation, his wounded feet, his healing hands, his pierced heart which has become a door open for others.[105]

I cannot solve the problem of innocent suffering. In the end, like Paul and Job, I can only throw myself on the mercy of God.

To conclude, I believe that after the Holocaust we should no longer define ourselves as Christians against the other, Judaism. Rather, acknowledging our common sinfulness *(this, to my mind, is the punchline of Romans 1–3, placed at Romans 2:1)* and the universal mercy of God *(Romans 11:32, the punchline of Romans 9–11)*, we should understand ourselves as brothers and sisters, as all being sinners under the mercy of God.[106]

In the parable of the prodigal son, the Father, standing for God, loves and invites the response of both sons, the prodigal son and

---

[105] Gervase Vernon. A broken heart is a door open for others. Br J Gen Pract. 2020 Apr 30;70(694):243 s.

[106] Sheldon Vanauken. *Under the Mercy*. Hodder & Stoughton Religious,1985. In *A severe mercy*, a favourite book of mine, the author, Sheldon Vanauken, a disciple of C. S. Lewis, tries to come to terms with the death of his wife at a young age. 'Under the mercy' was the sequel. Vanauken may have meant, 'under the mercy but not under the Law' referring to Romans. The phrase, 'under the mercy' he borrowed from Charles Williams.
http://oxfordinklings.blogspot.com/2007/03/under-mercy.html

the elder brother. He condemns neither, but goes out to both of them and invites a response. So God still loves and invites a response from the two surviving religious traditions which trace their origins back to Second Temple Judaism; rabbinical Judaism and Christianity. As Pope Francis sets out in the quotation above, both traditions are witness to God's love and faithfulness.

Questions

1) What do you think of this interpretation of Romans 9–11? There are plenty of others.

2) What have you learnt from the course about Christians and Jews?

3) How will it alter your outlook and behaviour in the future?

4) *Is there any occasion we can remember where we have been perceived as 'the other' and suffered because of it?*

5) *Can we remember any occasion when we have welcomed the other? Has it brought us joy?*

6) *Does your church, or has your church, ever excluded the other? How can we repent of this?*

7) *How can you make your church more inclusive, more welcoming of 'the other'?*

Postscript

In 'East-West Street' Phillipe Sands (location 2190)[107] describes how his mother, aged one, was brought from Vienna to Paris in 1940 by a Miss Elsie Tilney. Miss Tilney turns out to have been a very brave Protestant missionary from Norfolk who not only saved the life of Phillipe Sand's mother but at least one other Jew, hiding him for six months in an internment camp in Vittel, France. When Phillipe searches for her motivation, others from the same chapel point him to Romans 10:1 'brothers, my heart's desire and prayer to God is for Israel, that they may be saved'. (Also Romans 1:16, 'for the Jew first' which was the motto of the 'Surrey Chapel' to which she belonged.) He sees her as motivated by both religion and compassion.

---

[107] Philippe Sands QC. *East West Street: on the origins of genocide and crimes against humanity*: Weidenfeld & Nicolson, 2016.

Sources

1) Tom Wright. Paul for Everyone: Romans Part 1 and Part II. SPCK, 2006.

2) Rowan Williams. Meeting God in Paul. SPCK, 2015.

3) Amy-Jill Levine, Marc Zvi Brettler (editors). The Jewish Annotated New Testament. OUP USA, 2017.

4) Raymond Brown. *An Introduction to the New Testament.* Yale University Press, 2007.

5) Elie Wiesel. *Night.* Penguin Classics, 2006.

6) Jürgen Moltmann. Jewish and Christian theologies after Auschwitz. 'Common Ground' magazine of the Council of Christians and Jews. Autumn 2021 pp. 6–11.

7) Jürgen Moltmann. *The crucified God.* SCM classics 2001.

The definitive resource in English at the present time is:

8) N.T. Wright. Paul and the Faithfulness of God. SPCK, 2013.

This long study of Paul, which I have not read, devotes more than a hundred pages to a careful, step-by-step interpretation of Romans 9–11 (1156-1258).

See also:

Richard Breitman. *Official Secrets: What the Nazis Planned, What the British and Americans Knew.* Farrar, Straus & Giroux, 1998. ISBN 0-8090-3819-6

7. WEEK 5B. THE TEXT OF ROMANS 9-11 FROM THE NRSV

Normal type rejoices the gentiles, *italics rejoices the Jews,* **the bold is Paul's synthesis.**[108]

God's Election of Israel

9 *I am speaking the truth in Christ—I am not lying; my conscience confirms it by the Holy Spirit— ² I have great sorrow and unceasing anguish in my heart. ³ For I could wish that I myself were accursed and cut off from Christ for the sake of my own people,[a] my kindred according to the flesh. ⁴ They are Israelites, and to them belong the adoption, the glory[109], the covenants, the giving of the law, the*

---

[108] I have used bold and italic types because this booklet is printed in black and white. If printed out for an audience or displayed on a screen, colours are better. For example: Normal type (Blue) rejoices the gentiles, italics (red) rejoices the Jews, the bold (green) is Paul's synthesis.

[109] The glorious divine presence in the Jerusalem temple (Paula Fredriksen, Jewish Annotated NT loc 33861)

worship[110], and the promises; **5** to them belong the patriarchs, and from them, according to the flesh, comes the Messiah,[b] who is over all, God blessed forever.[111][c] Amen.[112]

God has kept his promise

6 It is not as though the word of God had failed. For not all Israelites truly belong to Israel, **7** and not all of Abraham's children are his true descendants, but "It is through Isaac that descendants shall be named for you." **8** This means that it is not the children of the flesh who are the children of God, but the children of the promise are counted as descendants. **9** For this is what the promise said, "About this time I will return and Sarah shall have a son." **10** Nor is that all, something similar happened to Rebecca when she had conceived children by one husband, our ancestor Isaac. **11** Even before they had been born or had done anything good or bad (so that God's purpose of election might continue, **12** not by works but by his call) she was told, "The elder shall serve the younger." **13** As it is written,

"I have loved Jacob,

but I have hated Esau."

---

[110] Latreia, the sacrificial cult

[111] Jewish 'according to the flesh', but also Lord of all. (Tom Wright). See Romans 1:3-4.

[112] Is this the earliest reference to Jesus as God in the NT (Brown)

God is not unjust.

⁴ What then are we to say? Is there injustice on God's part? By no means! ¹⁵ For he says to Moses,

"I will have mercy on whom I have mercy,
   and I will have compassion on whom I have compassion."

¹⁶ So it depends not on human will or exertion, but on God who shows mercy. ¹⁷ For the scripture says to Pharaoh, "I have raised you up for the very purpose of showing my power in you, so that my name may be proclaimed in all the earth." ¹⁸ So then he has mercy on whomever he chooses, and he hardens the heart of whomever he chooses.

¹⁹ You will say to me then, "Why then does he still find fault? For who can resist his will?" ²⁰ But who indeed are you, a human being, to argue with God? Will what is moulded say to the one who moulds it, "Why have you made me like this?" ²¹ Has the potter no right over the clay, to make out of the same lump one object for special use and another for ordinary use?[113] ²² What if God, desiring to show his wrath and to make known his power, has endured with much patience the objects of

---

[113] Isaiah 29:16, 45:9, 64:8, Jeremiah 18:1-6.

wrath that are made for destruction, ²³ and what if he has done so in order to make known the riches of his glory for the objects of mercy, which he has prepared beforehand for glory— ²⁴ <u>including us whom he has called, not from the Jews only but also from the Gentiles?</u>

As has been foretold in the Old Testament, God calls a remnant.

(Israel's story so far The Exile and the return from Babylon)

²⁵ As indeed he says in Hosea,

"Those who were not my people I will call 'my people,'
    and her who was not beloved I will call 'beloved.'"[114]
²⁶ "And in the very place where it was said to them, 'You are not my people,'
    there they shall be called children of the living God."[115]

---

[114] Hosea 2:23
[115] Hosea 1:10

27 And Isaiah cries out concerning Israel, "Though the number of the children of Israel were like the sand of the sea, only a remnant of them will be saved; **28** for the Lord will execute his sentence on the earth quickly and decisively."[116] **29** And as Isaiah predicted,

"If the Lord of hosts had not left survivors[e] to us,
  we would have fared like Sodom
  and been made like Gomorrah."[117]

Israel's Unbelief

30 What then are we to say? Gentiles, who did not strive for righteousness, have attained it, that is, <u>righteousness through faith</u>, **31** but Israel, who did strive for the righteousness that is based on the law, did not succeed in fulfilling that law. **32** Why not? <u>Because they did not strive for it on the basis of faith, but as if it were based on works</u>. They have stumbled over the stumbling stone, **33** as it is written,

"See, I am laying in Zion a stone that will make people stumble, a rock that will make them fall, and whoever believes in him[f] will not be put to shame."[118]

---

[116] Isaiah 10:22, Genesis 2:17
[117] Isaiah 1:9
[118] Isaiah 28:16, Isaiah 8:14

Israel fails to see that it is God who makes us holy

10 *Brothers and sisters,* [g] *my heart's desire and prayer to God for them is that they may be saved.* **2** *I can testify that they have a zeal for God, but it is not enlightened.* **3** For, being ignorant of the righteousness that comes from God, and seeking to establish their own, they have not submitted to God's righteousness. **4** <u>For Christ is the end of the law so that there may be righteousness for everyone who believes.</u>

The fulfilment of the 'New Covenant' promised by Moses (in Deuteronomy 30) is for all

5 *Moses writes concerning the righteousness that comes from the law, that "the person who does these things will live by them."* **6 But the righteousness that comes from faith says, "Do not say in your heart, 'Who will ascend into heaven?'" (that is, to bring Christ down) 7 "or 'Who will descend into the abyss?'" (that is, to bring Christ up from the dead). 8 But what does it say?**

"The word is near you,
  on your lips and in your heart"[119]

---

[119] Deuteronomy 30:12-14. Deuteronomy 30 contains God's promise of a renewed covenant, of a circumcision of the heart, after return from exile. For

(that is, the word of faith that we proclaim), ⁹ <u>because</u>[h] <u>if you confess with your lips that Jesus is Lord</u>[120] <u>and believe in your heart that God raised him from the dead, you will be saved.</u> ¹⁰ For one believes with the heart and so is justified, and one confesses with the mouth and so is saved. ¹¹ The scripture says, "No one who believes in him will be put to shame."[121] ¹² <u>For there is no distinction between Jew and Greek; the same Lord is Lord of all and is generous to all who call on him.</u>¹³ For, "Everyone who calls on the name of the Lord shall be saved."[122]

Israel has no excuse. *(All have heard God's word through creation. Israel's failure to recognise the Messiah had been predicted by Moses.)*

¹⁴ But how are they to call on one in whom they have not believed? And how are they to believe in one of whom they have never heard? And how are they to hear without someone to proclaim him? ¹⁵ And how are they to proclaim him unless they are sent?[123] As it is written, "How beautiful are the feet of those who bring good news!"[124] ¹⁶ But not all have obeyed the good news;[ii] for Isaiah says, "Lord, who has

---

Paul this new covenant is given in Jesus. (Tom Wright).
[120] 'Confessing that Jesus is Lord', is what people did at baptism (Tom Wright)
[121] Isaiah 28:16 as at Romans 9:33
[122] Joel 2:32

[124] Isaiah 52.7

believed our message?"[125] [17] So faith comes from what is heard, and what is heard comes through the word of Christ.[ii]

[18] But I ask, have they not heard? Indeed they have; for

"Their voice has gone out to all the earth,
and their words to the ends of the world."[126]

[19] Again I ask, did Israel not understand? First Moses says,

"I will make you jealous of those who are not a nation;
with a foolish nation I will make you angry."[127]

[20] Then Isaiah is so bold as to say,

"I have been found by those who did not seek me;
I have shown myself to those who did not ask for me."[128]

[21] But of Israel he says, "All day long I have held out my hands to a disobedient and contrary people."[129]

---

[125] Isaiah 53:1. Part of the fourth song of the servant.

[126] Psalm 19:4, a psalm which proclaims that all can know God through his creation. Natural theology as in Romans 1:18-20 or Colossians 1:23.

[127] Deuteronomy 32:21, a part of the 'Song of Moses' which closely follows the covenant promises of Deuteronomy 30. Paul is claiming that the failure of Israel to recognise the Messiah had been predicted by Moses. (Tom Wright)

[128] Isaiah 65:1. Isaiah 65 is a prophecy of the coming judgement.

[129] Isaiah 65:2

Israel's Rejection Is Not Final

1) A remnant of Israel is saved

11 *I ask, then, has God rejected his people? By no means! I myself am an Israelite, a descendant of Abraham, a member of the tribe of Benjamin. ² God has not rejected his people[130] whom he foreknew. Do you not know what the scripture says of Elijah, how he pleads with God against Israel? ³ "Lord, they have killed your prophets, they have demolished your altars; I alone am left, and they are seeking my life." ⁴ But what is the divine reply to him? "I have kept for myself seven thousand who have not bowed the knee to Baal." ⁵ So too at the present time there is a remnant, chosen by grace. ⁶ But if it is by grace, it is no longer on the basis of works, otherwise grace would no longer be grace.*[k]

2) A stumble with a purpose

⁷ What then? Israel failed to obtain what it was seeking. The elect obtained it, but the rest were hardened, **⁸** as it is written,

"God gave them a sluggish spirit,
   eyes that would not see

---

[130] 1 Samuel 12:22. From the passage where Samuel makes Saul king.

and ears that would not hear,

down to this very day."[131]

9 And David says,

"Let their table become a snare and a trap,

　　a stumbling block and a retribution for them;

10 let their eyes be darkened so that they cannot see,

　　and keep their backs forever bent."[132]

The Salvation of the Gentiles and the future restoration of Israel

11 So I ask, have they stumbled so as to fall? By no means! But through their stumbling[l] salvation has come to the Gentiles[133], so as to make Israel[m] jealous.[134] 12 Now if their stumbling[n] means riches for the world, and if their defeat means riches for Gentiles, how much more will their full inclusion mean!

13 Now I am speaking to you Gentiles.[135] Inasmuch then as I am an apostle to the Gentiles, I glorify my

---

[131] Deuteronomy 29:3-4

[132] Psalm 69:22-23

[133] The theme of people meaning evil, but God using it for good, is how Joseph forgives his brothers (Genesis 50:20).

[134] The theme of jealousy between two brothers flows through the book of Genesis and is the background for the parable of the prodigal son.

[135] 'Speaking to you gentiles.' Is this an indication that the whole letter is to a gentile church, or that this passage is addressed to gentiles? See Romans 1:6.

ministry[14] in order to make my own people[o] jealous,[136] and thus save some of them.[15] For if their rejection is the reconciliation of the world, <u>what will their acceptance be but life from the dead!</u>[137]

Israel is still the chosen people, the two olive trees

[16] *If the part of the dough offered as first fruits is holy, then the whole batch is holy and if the root is holy, then the branches also are holy.[138]*

[17] *But if some of the branches were broken off, and you, a wild olive shoot, were grafted in their <u>place to share the rich root</u>[p] <u>of the [cultivated] olive tree [Israel],</u>[18] <u>do not boast</u> over the branches.[139] If you do boast, remember that <u>it is not you that supports the root, but the root that supports you.</u> [19] You will say, "Branches were broken off so that I might be grafted in." [20] That is true. They were broken off because of their unbelief, but you stand only through faith. So <u>do not become proud, but stand in awe</u>. [21] For if God did not spare the natural branches, perhaps he will not spare you.[q] [22] **Note then the**

---

[136] Literally, 'making my flesh jealous'

[137] Just as the rejection of Jesus lead to the resurrection (Tom Wright).

[138] Those Jews who already follow Christ are the first fruits, in some way, they make all Israel holy (Tom Wright).

[139] If the gentile Christ followers boast that they have replaced Israel, this will put off the Jews from recognising Jesus as Messiah and thus harm God's plans for the eventual conversion of Israel. Mark D. Nanos. Jewish annotated NT.

kindness and the severity of God: severity towards those who have fallen, but God's kindness towards you, provided you continue in his kindness, otherwise, you also will be cut off. [23] And even those of Israel,[ɪ] if they do not persist in unbelief[140], will be grafted in, for God has the power to graft them in again. [24] For if you have been cut from what is by nature a wild olive tree and grafted, contrary to nature,[141] into a cultivated olive tree, how much more will these natural branches be grafted back into their own olive tree.

The final conversion of the Israelites

[25] **So that you may not claim to be wiser than you are**, brothers and sisters,[142] I want you to understand this mystery: a hardening has come upon part of Israel, until the full number of the Gentiles has come in. [26] **And so all Israel will be saved**[143]; as it is written,

---

[140] Apistia, lack of steadfastness, unbelief

[141] Normally a branch of a cultivated olive tree would be grafted onto a wild olive.

[142] Paul is here calling the gentile Christians, as well as the Jews, 'his brothers' for the first time (Tom Wright).

[143] Is Paul here referring to the descendants of Israel by the flesh, or descendants of Abraham by faith (Romans 4:9)? (Tom Wright believes the latter).

"Out of Zion will come the Deliverer;
  he will banish ungodliness from Jacob."
[27] "And this is my covenant with them,
  when I take away their sins."[144]

[28] As regards the gospel they are enemies of God[ɯ] for your sake, *but as regards election they are beloved, for the sake of their ancestors;[145]* **[29]** *for the gifts and the calling of God are irrevocable.* **[30]** *Just as you were once disobedient to God but have now received mercy because of their disobedience, [31] so they have now been disobedient in order that, by the mercy shown to you, they too may now[146] receive mercy.* **[32] For God has imprisoned all in disobedience so that he may be merciful to all.**

A Hymn to God's Mercy and wisdom

[33] O the depth of the riches and wisdom and knowledge of God! How unsearchable are his judgments and how inscrutable his ways!

---

[144] A synthesis of Isaiah 59:20-21, Jeremiah 31:33-34 and Isaiah 27:9.
[145] The translation of Romans 11:28 is controversial. The NIV version, 'As far as the gospel is concerned, they are enemies for your sake; but as far as election is concerned, they are loved on account of the patriarchs,' is to be preferred. The Greek original does not have the phrase, 'enemies of God' but does have 'enemies of the Gospel'. Thanks to Claire Malone-Lee for pointing this out.
[146] The conversion of Israel is starting 'now'.

³⁴ "For who has known the mind of the Lord?

   Or who has been his counsellor?"

³⁵ "Or who has given a gift to him,

   to receive a gift in return?"[147]

³⁶ For from him and through him and to him are all things. To him be the glory forever. Amen.[148]

---

[147] Job 41:11. Jerusalem Bible 41:32 has a different translation.
[148] The final aim of God's creation, already securely underway in Jesus (Tom Wright).

8 Postscript; a brief history

For those who are interested, I have included in this postscript a brief history of Judaism, and a history of the engagement with secular philosophy of both religions: Judaism and Christianity.

1. A very brief history of Judaism

The Jewish religion has a long history. That form of Judaism which was most prevalent between the restoration of the Jerusalem temple by Ezra and Nehemiah (circa 516 BCE) and the destruction of this second, restored temple by the Romans in 70 CE is called Second Temple Judaism.[149] To this belonged the Pharisees, the Sadducees, the High Priests, Jesus, John the Baptist and Paul. This form of Judaism was centred on the temple where daily sacrifices were offered. Most sacrifices concerned ritual purity and were not

---

[149] The community that wrote the Dead Sea Scrolls was highly critical of Second Temple Judaism.

sin offerings.[150] There were a large number of priests.[151] Jews throughout the Roman empire paid a ten per cent tax to the temple in Jerusalem, contributing to making Jerusalem the largest city in the East of the Roman empire until its destruction.[152]

All this came to an abrupt end with the destruction of the Jerusalem temple and Jerusalem itself by the Romans in AD 70. Only two religious traditions alive today trace themselves back to Second Temple Judaism; rabbinic Judaism and Christianity. Both these traditions look back to the Pharisees, that current of Second Temple Judaism which believed in the resurrection of the dead and which took seriously not only the written Law – the Torah (the first five books of the Hebrew Scriptures) but also the 'oral law', handed down by the elders, which would be later codified in the Mishnah. In contrast, the Sadducees did not believe in the resurrection of the dead, angels or spirits (Acts 23:8).

Other streams of Judaism petered out. After the fall of Jerusalem, there remained a large community of Jews in Alexandria. They had given the Greek world a translation of the Hebrew scriptures, the Septuagint. Philo, an Alexandrian Jew, a rough contemporary of Jesus, attempted to harmonise the Torah to Greek philosophy. There were Jewish kingdoms among the Khazars in the Crimea in

---

[150] As, for example, the pair of doves offered by Joseph and Mary after Jesus's birth (Luke 2:23-24).

[151] J. Jeremias, *Jerusalem in the Time of Jesus*. Bunko, 1969. Jeremias estimates 18000 priests.

[152] Simon Sebag Montefiore. *Jerusalem: The Biography*. W&N, 2020.

the eighth century[153] and in Yemen (circa 380–520)[154]. But none of these had a lasting influence on Rabbinic Judaism which instead was founded by those rabbis who escaped the destruction of Jerusalem and then established academies in Yavne in Palestine and later other academies such as that at Pumbedita near Babylon. Rabbinic Judaism, founded by these Rabbis, codified the oral law as the Mishnah. Commentaries on the Mishna (which are called Gemara) formed, together with the Mishna itself, the Talmud. The two different versions of the Talmud are called the Jerusalem and Babylonian Talmud. The commentaries in the Talmud are divided into Halakha, commentaries on the Law, and Aggadah, stories often with an ethical, theological or philosophical meaning.

The Karaites, communities who rejected the oral Torah and the Talmud, may have been as numerous as rabbinic Jews in the eleventh century, and continued in reasonable numbers until WWII. Many scholars believe that they gave us the Masoretic text of the OT, which Jews and Christians still use today.

Rabbinic Judaism, just like Christianity, has a two-thousand-year history. Like Christianity it split into many streams which competed with each other. In a book of this length, it would not be possible to deal with every stream of either tradition. For

---

[153] https://en.wikipedia.org/wiki/Khazars
See also, Arthur Koestler. *The Thirteenth Tribe: The Khazar Empire and its Heritage.* One 70 Press, 1976.
[154] *Histoire du Coran editors Mohammad Ali Amir-Moezzi et Guillaume Dye.* Les Editions du Cerf, 2022.
Chap. 1 Christian Julien Robin. Le Coran et les débuts de l'islam.

Christianity, I have mainly referred to my own Roman Catholic tradition, but with frequent mention of Anglican positions. For Rabbinic Judaism, my dialogue has been with the written works of Rabbi Jonathan Sachs, who represents Orthodox Judaism. I have chosen to concentrate on this stream of Judaism because of its obvious continuity with Rabbinic Judaism in previous generations and because Jonathan Sacks was both a marvellous writer and widely respected throughout the Jewish community and beyond.

Note: For those who would like more detail on the history of Judaism, a textbook which provides a history of Jewish religion and tradition from a Reform Judaism perspective is:

Dan Cohn-Sherbok. *The Jewish Heritage*. Basil Blackwell, 1988.

2. Religion and philosophy.

In both the Christian tradition, and that of Rabbinic Judaism, there has been a dialogue between the revealed truths of religion and secular philosophy throughout their two-thousand-year history. This dialogue, in both traditions, has ranged from acceptance of contemporary secular philosophy to complete its rejection. This dialogue continues today.

From a Jewish perspective, Philo (c. 20 BCE–c. 50 CE), as already mentioned, engaged with Hellenistic culture. Maimonides (1138–1204), in his 'Guide for the perplexed' engaged with the philosophy of Aristotle. The 'perplexed' of the titled are not uneducated Jews, but those learned Jews whose study of Aristotle has perplexed them. There was a strong reaction against Maimonides by some scholars, led by Solomon ben Abraham of Montpellier (first half of the thirteenth century) and a rejection of Aristotelianism in the works of Nachmanides (1194–1270).

The Haskalah, the Jewish enlightenment, engaged with European enlightenment (1770s to 1880s), and was a predecessor of current Reform Judaism. The Misnagdim, mainly based in Lithuania, emphasized the study of the Law. They are one of the sources of modern Orthodox Judaism. The Hasidim (mid-18th-c. to today)[155], mainly based in Southern Poland, were more charismatic and less intellectual. Both Misnagdim and Hasidim strongly rejected the Haskalah, the Jewish enlightenment and involvement with surrounding gentile culture.

On the Christian side, Justin Martyr (c. AD 100–c. AD 165) wrote that Christianity was present in embryo in Greek philosophy, while Tertullian (c. AD 155–c. AD 220) fought fiercely against any engagement with secular wisdom, writing, 'What has Athens to do with Jerusalem?' Augustine, who had received a classical Roman education, was much more willing to engage with the culture of the Roman empire. Thomas Aquinas (1225–1274), writing after Maimonides, formed a synthesis of Aristotelian philosophy and Christian revelation which is still dominant in the Roman Catholic church today. The Protestant reformer Luther (1483–1546) sought

---

[155] Hasidism is a social and religious movement, started in Southern Poland, which emphasized that God is accessible to all Jews.

to return to 'scripture alone'. Calvin (1509–1564) proved more welcoming to modern science than the Roman Catholic church of his day, refusing to censor the theories of Copernicus. David F. Ford in his book places contemporary Christian theologians in different categories depending on the way in which they engage with a particular modern philosophical viewpoint, some accepting a particular philosophy entirely, some in dialogue with different philosophies, some fiercely rejecting all modern philosophy.[156]

Finally one could consider the dialogue between Christianity and Judaism, which is covered in more detail in week four of this book. Here there is an oscillation between prolonged periods of deep antagonism and short moments of openness. Jerome, who translated the Bible into Latin, the translation known as the Vulgate, had close relations with Jewish scholars in Palestine. Pico della Mirandola (1463–1494) was a Christian humanist much inspired by the Jewish thinkers of his time. The current Pope, Francis I, is a friend of, and wrote a book with, an Argentinian Rabbi, Abraham Skorka. [157]

For both Jews and Christians, the scriptures are inspired by God.[158] But God had to have them written in a way that was comprehensible to the people who first received them, people who

---

[156] David F. Ford. *Theology: A Very Short Introduction*. Oxford University Press, 1999. Chapter 2, p.27.

[157] Pope Francis and Abraham Skorka. On Heaven and Earth. Image, 2013.

[158] Various approaches to the knotty questions of the inspiration and revelation are well described and evaluated in Raymond Brown. *An introduction the New Testament*. Doubleday, 1997. Chapter 2.

lived in a world quite different from our own. The interpretation of these sacred scriptures for the people of later times has been an inescapable part of the work of scholars, priests and rabbis ever since. How come well-meaning and learned scholars, Christians on the one hand and Jews on the other, studying the same texts, come to such different interpretations? This is a painful mystery over which Paul agonises in Romans chapters 9–11 (see week 5) and over which many have agonised since. But is the distinction between the traditions really that great? Both traditions agree on the depiction of God in the Hebrew scriptures, a God who reconciles compassion and justice. Every ethical precept of the New Testament can be found in the Hebrew scriptures.[159] While both traditions await the arrival of the Messiah, the major difference is that Christians expect to recognise the Messiah, when he returns, from his previous incarnation as Jesus.[160]

---

[159] An exception could be made for those passages in the NT where we are urged to 'imitate Jesus', for example John 13:34 where we are given a new commandment to love as Jesus loved us.

[160] Christians, who believe that Jesus was the Messiah, have a different view of the ritual provisions of the Torah from Rabbinical Judaism. Nevertheless, Christians have a wide range of views; from Matthew, who wrote that Jesus fulfilled the Law (Matthew 5:17), to Paul for whom the Law has, in some translations of Ephesians 2:15, been abolished, (though, in the Greek, according to some literal translations, it may be the enmity between Greek and Jew due to the Law that has been abolished). Either way, once the Messiah has come, one can accept that some change in the status of the Law is likely to occur.

9 Bibliography

The following is a list of books and other resources for those who wish to take things further. It is not an index to all the books referred to in the text.

There are more exhaustive lists on specific topics at the end of Chapter 5 (The Holocaust and Christian anti-Judaism) and Chapter 4 (Bobowa and the Shoah).

General works

The Jewish Annotated New Testament. Amy-Jill Levine (Editor), Marc Z. Brettler (Editor). OUP, USA, 2017.

Edward Kessler. *An Introduction to Jewish-Christian Relations*. Cambridge University Press, 2010.

John Connelly. *From Enemy to Brother: The Revolution in Catholic Teaching on the Jews, 1933–1965*. Harvard University Press, 2008.

The works of Jonathan Sacks

Rabbi Jonathan Sacks. *Not in God's Name: Confronting Religious Violence*. London. Hodder and Stoughton, 2016.

Jonathan Sacks. *Genesis, the Book of Beginnings (v. 1) (Covenant and Conversation)*. Toby Press, 2010.

Jonathan Sacks. *Covenant & Conversation Exodus: The Book of Redemption*. Toby Press, 2010.

These commentaries on the Torah can mostly be found online at:

https://www.rabbisacks.org/covenant-conversation/

There are also many videos of Rabbi Sacks at:

https://www.rabbisacks.org/videos/animations/

Finally, a video of Jonathan Sacks addressing the 2008 Lambeth conference:

https://www.rabbisacks.org/videos/faith-and-fate-the-lambeth-conference-address/

Other books and resources, (see also the bibliography at the end of Chapter 5)

2010. Karl Rahner and Pinchas Lapide. *Encountering Jesus – Encountering Judaism*. Crossroads, New York, 1987.

Sisters of Our Lady of Sion. On their website are recordings of many wonderful talks: https://sioncentre.org/

The 'International Council of Christians and Jews' has an on-line magazine 'Jewish Christian relations' at

https://www.iccj.org/article/jcrelationsnet-may-edition-online-8-1.html

About Scriptural reasoning

David F. Ford. *The Promise of Scriptural Reasoning*. Ed. with C. C. Pecknold. With the chapter 'An Inter-Faith Wisdom: Scriptural Reasoning between Jews, Christians and Muslims' at pp. 1–22 (Blackwell, Oxford, 2006)

Jews, Christians and Muslims Meet around their Scriptures: An Inter-faith Practice for the 21st Century David F. Ford, Regius Professor of Divinity and Director of the Cambridge Inter-faith Programme, University of Cambridge. The Fourth Pope John Paul II Annual Lecture on Interreligious Understanding. The Pontifical University of St Thomas Aquinas 'Angelicum' with The Russell Berrie Foundation. Rome, April 5th 2011.

This lecture can be found at:

https://www.interfaith.cam.ac.uk/resources/lecturespapersandspeeches/jewschristiansandmuslimsmeetaroundtheirscriptures

10 Mean, angry Old Testament God vs. Nice, loving New Testament God?

(by Eva Mroczek and others) [161]

...not so fast. This is a common stereotype! Yes, parts of the Hebrew Bible (Old Testament) depict divine wrath, while parts of the New Testament show divine love and forgiveness.

But there are THREE reasons this stereotype is wrong.

1.   It emphasizes some texts, but ignores many others.

IT'S VERY EASY TO USE TEXTUAL EVIDENCE TO MAKE THE EXACT OPPOSITE ARGUMENT!
We can find plenty of love and mercy in the HB/OT, and lots of violence and vengeance in the NT:

DIVINE LOVE AND MERCY IN THE HB/OT	DIVINE WRATH AND VIOLENCE IN THE NT
God is compassionate and slow to anger:	*Jesus says he has come to sow violence:* 'Do not think that I have come to bring peace to the earth; I have not come to bring peace, but a

[161] by Eva Mroczek and others, see the end for full authorship. From: https://docs.google.com/document/d/1BG5PvCO5pTTATcgBFDa5j9p0myFgg9 wj1ECkrRhFbl/edit?pli=1

"The Lord, the Lord, the compassionate and gracious God, slow to anger, abounding in love and faithfulness" (Exodus 34:6).	sword. I have come to set a man against his father, and a daughter against her mother, and a daughter-in-law against her mother-in-law; and one's foes will be members of one's own household' (Mt 10: 34-39).
God gently cares for all plants and animals: 10 [God] makes springs pour water into the ravines; it flows between the mountains. 11 They give water to all the beasts of the field; the wild donkeys quench their thirst. 12 The birds of the sky nest by the waters; they sing among the branches. 13 He waters the mountains from his upper chambers; the land is satisfied by the fruit of his work. 14 He makes grass grow for the cattle, and plants for people to cultivate— bringing forth food from the earth: 15 wine that gladdens human hearts, oil to make their faces shine, and bread that sustains their hearts. 16 The trees of the Lord are well watered, the cedars of Lebanon that he planted (Ps 104).	*Jesus curses a fig tree because he's hangry:* [Jesus] was hungry. Seeing in the distance a fig tree in leaf, he went to see whether perhaps he would find anything on it. When he came to it, he found nothing but leaves, for it was not the season for figs. He said to it, 'May no one ever eat fruit from you again.' And his disciples heard it (Mark 11: 12-14).
God is a gentle shepherd who carries people in his arms like baby animals:	*God will torture sinners forever even after death:* When the Lord Jesus is revealed from heaven with his mighty angels in flaming fire, inflicting

He tends his flock like a shepherd: He gathers the lambs in his arms and carries them close to his heart; he gently leads those that have young. (Isaiah 40:11)	vengeance on those who do not know God and on those who do not obey the gospel of our Lord Jesus. These will suffer the punishment of eternal destruction, separated from the presence of the Lord and from the glory of his might (2 Thess 1:7-9).
God requires love and equal treatment for all, regardless of where they are from: "The stranger who resides with you shall be to you as one of your citizens; you shall love him as yourself" (Leviticus 19:34).	*Sinners are like yard waste - they'll be burned:* [Jesus's] disciples approached him, saying, 'Explain to us the parable of the weeds of the field.' He answered, 'The one who sows the good seed is the Son of Man; the field is the world, and the good seed are the children of the kingdom; the weeds are the children of the evil one, and the enemy who sowed them is the devil; the harvest is the end of the age, and the reapers are angels. Just as the weeds are collected and burned up with fire, so will it be at the end of the age. The Son of Man will send his angels, and they will collect out of his kingdom all causes of sin and all evildoers, and they will throw them into the furnace of fire, where there will be weeping and gnashing of teeth (Matthew 13:36-43).
God heals, protects, forgives, and does not judge people based on their sins: 2 Bless the Lord, O my soul, and do not forget all his benefits— 3 who forgives all your iniquity, who heals all your diseases, 4 who redeems your life from the Pit, who crowns you with steadfast love and mercy...	*On Judgement Day, God will condemn some people to suffer in a lake of fire forever:* Then I saw a great white throne and the one who sat on it; the earth and the heaven fled from his presence, and no place was found for them. And I saw the dead, great and small, standing before the throne, and books were opened. Also another book was opened, the book of life. And the dead were judged according to their works, as recorded in the books. And the sea gave up the dead that were in it, Death and Hades gave up the dead that were in them, and all were judged according to what they had done. Then Death and Hades

6 The Lord works vindication and justice for all who are oppressed.... 8 The Lord is merciful and gracious, slow to anger and abounding in steadfast love. 9 He will not always accuse, nor will he keep his anger forever. 10 He does not deal with us according to our sins, nor repay us according to our iniquities. 11 For as the heavens are high above the earth, so great is his steadfast love toward those who fear him... 13 As a father has compassion for his children, so the Lord has compassion for those who fear him (Ps. 103).	were thrown into the lake of fire. This is the second death, the lake of fire; and anyone whose name was not found written in the book of life was thrown into the lake of fire (Revelation 20: 11-15).

YIKES! Does this mean that God is actually loving and merciful in the Hebrew Bible, but vengeful in the New Testament?

NO. These examples are meant to illustrate that the "Angry OT God vs loving NT God" stereotype ignores lots of anger and violence in the New Testament, and lots of divine love and care in the Hebrew Bible. **BOTH anger and love are present** in **BOTH** the Hebrew Bible/OT and in the NT.

Identifying the HB/OT with anger and the NT with love doesn't reflect what's really there in the texts – **it is a result of pre-existing assumptions, commitments, and prejudices.**

But there's more!
2.   The stereotype overlooks the REASONS why God is often depicted as angry in the HB/OT:
        God is angry when vulnerable people are being oppressed.

God's anger is often directed at people who pretend to be pious, but **get rich by exploiting the poor** or **unjustly manipulating courts of law.**

Take this example from the Covenant Code in the Book of Exodus:

22 You shall not mistreat any widow or orphan. 23 If you do mistreat them, when they cry out to me, I will surely heed their cry; 24 my wrath will burn, and I will kill you with the sword, and your wives shall become widows and your children orphans. 25 If you lend money to my people, to the poor among you, you shall not deal with them as a creditor; you shall not exact interest from them. 26 If you take your neighbour's cloak in pawn, you shall restore it before the sun goes down; 27 for it may be your neighbour's only clothing to use as cover; in what else shall that person sleep? And if your neighbour cries out to me, I will listen, for I am compassionate (Exodus 22:22-27).

Here, God is very angry with those who take advantage of the poor and vulnerable, including predatory money-lenders, but is compassionate towards those they have harmed.

Or this one, from the Prophet Amos:

Ch. 2:6 They sell the innocent for silver, and the needy for a pair of sandals...
7 They trample on the heads of the poor as on the dust of the ground, and deny justice to the oppressed... Father and son use the same girl, and so profane my holy name.
8 They lie down beside every altar on garments taken in pledge. In the house of their god they drink wine taken as fines.
Ch. 5:10 There are those who hate the one who upholds justice in court, and detest the one who tells the truth... 11 You levy a straw tax on the poor and impose a tax on their grain.
Therefore, though you have built stone mansions, you will not live in them; though you have planted lush vineyards, you will not drink their wine.
12 For I know how many are your offences and how great your sins.
There are those who oppress the innocent and take bribes and deprive the poor of justice in the courts.
16 Therefore this is what the Lord, the Lord God Almighty, says:
"There will be wailing in all the streets and cries of anguish in every public square."

Here, God is angry at those who enrich themselves by exploiting the poor by imposing fines, levying taxes, repossessing their goods, and taking advantage of them in court. Here, God's anger will cause these oppressors to lose their wealth.

These same things elicit divine wrath and vengeance in the New Testament!

In the Gospel of Mark, Jesus condemns religious leaders who act pious, but get rich and famous by exploiting the poor – the same reason God is angry in the book of Amos:

> 38 They like to walk around in flowing robes and be greeted with respect in the marketplaces, 39 and have the most important seats in the synagogues and the places of honour at banquets. 40 They devour widows' houses and for a show make lengthy prayers. These men will be punished most severely (Mark 12:38-40).

Here's a different example from the community of Jesus-followers in the New Testament book of Acts. Members were required to sell their possessions and pool all their money together. One wealthy couple, Ananias and Saphira, sell their land, but only give *part* of the money to the collective, secretly keeping some of it for themselves. Both are immediately struck dead:

> 3 Then Peter said, "Ananias, how is it that Satan has so filled your heart that you have lied to the Holy Spirit and have kept for yourself some of the money you received for the land?... 5 When Ananias heard this, he fell down and died. [...] [Then]9 Peter said to [Saphira], "How could you conspire to test the Spirit of the Lord? Listen! The feet of the men who buried your husband are at the door, and they will carry you out also." 10 At that moment she fell down at his feet and died. 11 Great fear seized the whole church and all who heard about these events.

And finally:

3. Jesus DID say the greatest commandments are about love: to love God and love your neighbour!

But Jesus did not make this up – both come from the Hebrew Bible/OT, and love of God and neighbour are key for Jews as well.

> "You shall love your neighbour as yourself" (Leviticus 19:18)

As for the love of God, the Book of Deuteronomy says:

> Hear, O Israel: The Lord our God, the Lord is one. And you shall love the Lord your God with all your heart and with all your soul and with all your mind and with all your strength. (Deut 6:4)

In later Jewish practice, this became a prayer called the Shema ("Hear"), and is still **recited daily** by many Jews today.

Jewish teachers around Jesus's time taught the same thing about the most important teaching of the Torah. When the famous Rabbi Hillel was challenged to explain the whole Torah while standing on one foot, he said:

> "What is hateful to you, do not do to your neighbour. That is the entire Torah. The rest is commentary – go and learn." (Babylonian Talmud Shabbat 31a)

Handout prepared by Eva Mroczek with sources suggested by Matt Rindge, Ethan Schwartz, M Adryael Tong, and Meredith Warren, in collaboration with James Barker, Chance Bonar, Adam DJ Brett, Aaron Brody, Greg Carey, Julie Deluty, Angela Roskop Erisman, Chaya Halberstam, Diane Fruchtman Hannah, Martin Kavka, Sarah Kleeb, Barbara Krawcowicz, Lennart Lehmhaus, Shelly Matthews, Kelly Murphy, Sara Parks, Elliot Ratzman, Annette Yoshiko Reed, Kelsie Rodenbiker, Larry Wills. Special thanks to Mika Ahuvia for "Us vs. Them: Challenging Stereotypes about Judaism in the Wake of the Pittsburgh Shooting. Please retain this credit list if you use the handout, and indicate if it has been adapted :)

ABOUT THE AUTHOR

Dr Gervase Vernon is a retired general practitioner (family doctor). Among other books, he has written;

Belonging and Betrayal: Bronia's story. 2013. A fictionalized biography of his Russian Jewish grandmother.
The Lord's prayer; 'Our Father': An Ecumenical Commentary. 2020
The countenance of Christ: A commentary on the Beatitudes in Matthew. 2020
Looking at God looking at me: Collected essays and meditations on religious subjects. 2021
Bringing Saint Christopher back to Bobowa: Memories of childhood and youth, 1953 – 1984. 2023

These books are all independently published and exist as both paperback and Kindle versions.
'*Bringing Saint Christopher back to Bobowa*' contains a different version of Chater 4 of this book, 'Bobowa and the Shoah'. '*Looking at God looking at me*' contains an earlier version of Chapter 5, 'The Holocaust and Christian anti-Judaism'.

Printed in Great Britain
by Amazon